FIRE & Light

EUCHARISTIC
LOVE
AND
THE
SEARCH
FOR
PEACE

JACQUES PHILIPPE

Scepter

Contents

Introduction

The chapters of this book have various origins. Some were published as magazine articles, others have been adapted from lectures. They are presented here to make them more accessible to people as aids to living the Christian life.

The thread connecting them is a vision of Christian life as not primarily a tense and anxious human struggle, but a welcoming of God's gifts. Christianity is not a religion of human effort, but divine grace. To be sure, when the Church canonizes one of her children, she honors the beautiful response of that person to God's call. But she especially glorifies the mercy of the Father, the power that this mercy has in transforming a life. "For by grace you have been saved through faith; and this is not your own doing, it is the gift of God," says St. Paul (Eph 2:8).

To be Christian is not above all about fulfilling a task, a list of things to do. It is about welcoming, though faith (a faith entwined with hope and love), the immense gift offered freely to us. To live the gospel means learning to receive in our human heart, with its limits and weaknesses, all the richness of the Father's merciful love, letting ourselves be transformed by it day after day, responding freely and generously to it, and sharing it with those whom the Lord places on our path.

More than ever, God desires to reveal himself and to communicate himself to us. Nothing can give him more joy than to find hearts that welcome, with absolute trust and complete availability, the ceaselessly renewed gift of his love. May this book help its readers to persevere in faith, hope, and charity, to remain always open to the work of the Holy Spirit, and to hasten the Pentecost of love and mercy that God desires to spread across our world, so that "all flesh shall see the salvation of God," according to the promise of Scripture (Lk 3:6).

CHAPTER 1

Spiritual Receptivity

Learn to Receive

The most fundamental question of Christian life is this: How should we receive the grace of the Holy Spirit? How can we keep ourselves ever open to his action?

"The true aim of our Christian life consists of the acquisition of the Holy Spirit of God," said Seraphim of Sarov, one of the Russian Church's greatest saints, who died in 1833.[1] Fr. Marie-Eugene of the Child Jesus affirms: "Union with the Holy Spirit is not a luxury that belongs to the summit of spiritual life. . . . No, it is the first act, the first necessity."[2]

---

1. Emmanual Hatzidakis, *The Heavenly Banquet: Understanding the Divine Liturgy* (Clearwater, Fla.: Orthodox Witness, 2013), p. 280.

2. Father Marie-Eugene of the Child Jesus was a Discalced Carmelite friar and founder of the secular institute Notre Dame de Vie in Venasque, France. His beatification was announced by the Vatican in March 2016.

Indeed, without the grace of the Holy Spirit, we would not be able to do anything good or lasting. Jesus affirms that "apart from me you can do nothing" (Jn 15:5). Psalm 127 says the same: "Unless the Lord builds the house, those who build it labor in vain. Unless the Lord watches over the city, the watchman stays awake in vain" (Ps 127:1). Then the psalmist adds, with a bit of humor: "It is in vain that you rise up early and go late to rest, eating the bread of anxious toil; for he gives to his beloved sleep." Of course this does not mean we should spend our days in an armchair asking the Holy Spirit to do our work. The Spirit's action is no substitute for our human faculties, but it supports and directs them. One of the primary conditions for receiving the Holy Spirit is generosity in service and giving of ourselves; it is in giving that we receive.

The psalm reminds us, though, of something fundamental: if our mental reflections and our activities are not guided and sustained by divine grace, they are at high risk of remaining sterile. Sometimes we can exhaust ourselves with projects that produce nothing fruitful or long-lasting, because we act according to our own ideas and our own strength instead of being led by the Spirit.

There are lots of other reasons why opening up to the Spirit is so important. Only the Holy Spirit leads us to true freedom. "Where the Spirit of the Lord is, there is freedom," says St. Paul (2 Cor 3:17). Only the Holy Spirit makes us ceaselessly discover and deepen our true identity, that of children of God: "And because you are sons, God has sent the Spirit of his Son into our hearts, crying, 'Abba! Father!'" (Gal 4:6).

Some people feel that to be Christian means doing a number of things and the more we do, the better Christians we are. This does not reflect the Gospel at all. What is important in the Christian life is not to rush into a multitude of exterior works but to discover and to practice the attitudes and behaviors that open us up to the work of the Spirit. All the rest will flow from that, and we will be in a position to accomplish the "good works, which God prepared beforehand, that we should walk in them" (Eph 2:10). The spiritual life is not so much about *doing* as *letting be done*, letting God act in us, work through us.

Sometimes the Holy Spirit's action in our lives is perceptible; we feel its presence, its anointing. But often it is hidden. Sometimes, too, the Spirit enriches us with particular gifts: charisms, graces, inspirations, and the like. But sometimes it impoverishes us, making us aware of our radical insufficiency. We must not measure the presence and action of the Spirit according to superficial criteria.

It is sometimes perceptible, sometimes hidden, sometimes happy, sometimes sorrowful. But it matters little whether the Spirit's action is visible or not, consoling or challenging, for it is always fruitful. What counts is that we practice the attitudes that make us receptive to the Spirit's actions.

The Christian vocation calls us to give a lot. But to give a lot (without falling into fatigue, bitterness, or disillusion), it is necessary to learn to receive. "The merit doesn't consist in doing nor in giving a lot, but rather in receiving, in loving a lot," Thérèse of Lisieux said.[3]

We need to *learn to receive*. This is the most important, yet also sometimes the most difficult, part of the Christian existence.

We have difficulty giving because we are trapped in our own avarice, egoism, and fear. But we also often fail to receive. Even on a human level, it's sometimes easier to give than to receive, to love than to let ourselves be loved. Giving can stoke our pride: *I am the generous person who gives to others, who spends on them. . . .* Sometimes receiving is more difficult. It requires a kind of humility—recognizing that *I need the other person*—and

---

3. Thérèse of Lisieux, *Letters of St. Thérèse of Lisieux, Volume II: 1890–1897*, trans. John Clarke OCD (Washington, D.C.: ICS, 1988), LT 142. Kindle edition.

also demands confidence in others and openness to them, qualities that don't always come spontaneously.

All of this is to say that "to receive" isn't always as easy as we think. Yet it is the most fundamental act of the spiritual life. For we are creatures, and we depend totally on the Creator. We are also people who need to be saved and depend entirely on God's mercy, something we have difficulty admitting. In truth, we would all more or less consciously like to take the place of God as the sources of what we are and what we accomplish by ourselves. Let us understand that what is most necessary and most fruitful in human life is just the opposite—a welcoming attitude of receptiveness—even, I would say, of passivity.

It is vitally important to learn to receive, to receive one's very own self along with everything from God. To the extent we learn to receive everything from God, we can give to others the best of ourselves.

I will now describe the characteristics that seem to me to be the most important in guaranteeing a constant receptivity to the grace of the Holy Spirit. There are eight. This figure is of course somewhat arbitrary because we cannot divide the various aspects of the spiritual life into distinct slices, and someone could treat what I now propose to say differently. But it seems useful to group the different aspects of Christian life that permit openness to the Spirit's action under eight headings. These points are well-known, but I find it very helpful to look at them from the point of view of this receptivity upon which I insist so much. Each could be developed much more fully than I do here. I shall limit myself to what's essential, my intention being to provide an overview.

1. Perseverance in Prayer

Let's listen to the beautiful words of Jesus in Luke's Gospel: "Ask, and it will be given you; seek, and you will find; knock, and it will be opened to you. For every one who asks receives, and he who seeks finds, and to him who knocks it will be opened. What father among you, if his son asks for a fish, will instead of a fish give him a serpent; or if he asks for an egg, will give him a scorpion? If you then, who are evil, know how to give good gifts to your children, how much more will the heavenly Father give the Holy Spirit to those who ask him?" (Lk 11:9–13).

The first condition for receiving the Holy Spirit is, quite simply, to ask for it in prayer. Of course, this prayer must be driven by a great desire and much persevering. But it permits us to obtain what is necessary to carry out our Christian vocation. Perhaps the most consoling words in all of Scripture, I find, are these words of Jesus, "Ask, and you will receive." Confronted with our needs, our difficulties, Jesus invites us not to worry but simply to ask the Father for what we need, and he will give it. God hears the cry of the poor. Especially if one asks for this essential grace, which is the grace of the Holy Spirit.

Besides this prayer of asking, we should also faithfully practice silent prayer, which is essentially a prayer of receptivity. When we take time for personal prayer, for adoration—and this is absolutely indispensable, especially today—it's not time spent talking a lot, doing a lot, thinking a lot, but truly time given to welcoming God's presence in faith and love. The most deep and fruitful prayer is the prayer of pure receptivity.

Beyond the particular times that we consecrate to personal or community prayer, we do well to make our entire existence a conversation with God, following St. Paul's urging: "Pray at all times" (Eph 6:18). St. John of the Cross gives this advice: "Take God for your bridegroom and friend, and walk with him continually; and you will not sin and will learn to love, and the things you must do will work out prosperously for you."[4] All aspects

---

4. John of the Cross, *Sayings of Light and Love*, 65 in John of the Cross, *The Collected Works of St. John of the Cross*, trans. Kieran Kavanaugh, OCD, and Otilio Rodriguez, OCD (Washington, D.C.: ICS, 1991), 68. Kindle edition.

of our life can be nourished by this conversation with God: giving thanks for the beautiful things, calling on him in the face of difficult things, and even asking pardon for our faults. We should make everything fuel for the fire: for everything can feed and deepen our relationship with God, the good as well as the bad.

2. Trust

Trust is clearly an attitude of openness. We are welcoming and receptive insofar as we have trust. On the other hand, unbelief, doubt, suspicion, mistrust—these are closed-minded attitudes. The first thing God asks of us is not that we be perfect—it's to have confidence in him. What pains God the most is not our falls, but our lack of trust. The more we have confidence in him, the more we receive the Spirit. These are the words of Jesus to St. Faustina:

> The graces of My mercy are drawn by means of one vessel only, and that is—trust. The more a soul trusts, the more it will receive. Souls that trust boundlessly are a great comfort to Me, because I pour all the treasure of My graces into them. I rejoice that they ask for much, because it is My desire to give much, very

much. On the other hand, I am sad when souls ask for little, when they narrow their hearts.[5]

Trust and faith have an immense power to attract the grace of God. As Thérèse of Lisieux well understood, God has a father's heart and can't resist the filial trust of his children, particularly when it's a matter of granting them the forgiveness they so often need. In a letter to the abbot Bellière, she illustrates this with this little parable:

I would like to try to make you understand by means of a very simple comparison how much Jesus loves even imperfect souls who confide in him:

I picture a father who has two children, mischievous and disobedient, and when he comes to punish them, he sees one of them who trembles and gets away from him in terror, having, however, in the bottom of his heart the feeling that he deserves to be punished; and his brother, on the contrary, throws himself into his father's arms, saying that he is sorry for having caused him any trouble, that he loves him, and to prove it, he

---

5. Faustina Kowalska, *Diary of Saint Maria Faustina Kowalska: Divine Mercy in My Soul* (Stockbridge, Mass.: Marian Press, 2014), no. 1578.

will be good from now on. Then this child
asks his father *to punish* him with a *kiss*. I do
not believe that the heart of the happy father
could resist the filial confidence of his child,
whose sincerity and love he knows. He real-
izes, however, that more than once his son
will fall into the same faults, but he is prepared to pardon him always, if his son always
takes him by his heart. . . . I say nothing to
you about the first child, dear little Brother,
you must know whether his father can love
him as much and treat him with the same
indulgence as the other. . . .[6]

A decisive question about trust in God is this: On
what do we base our trust? Do we rely on ourselves
(our works, our accomplishments, our achievements),
which in the end is nothing other than trust in oneself?
Or does our confidence instead rest exclusively on God
and his infinite mercy? This means that even in poverty,
in failure and falls, trust remains firm. Genuine trust,
which is founded in God whose love never changes, is
practiced not only when all is well, when we are satisfied with ourselves, but also when we are faced with our

---

6. Thérèse of Lisieux, *Letters, Vol. II*, LT 258.

limitations and poverty. "If I had committed all possible crimes," said Thérèse, "I would always have the same confidence."[7]

3. Humility

Humility is also powerful in drawing to us the grace of the Holy Spirit. Listen to what Peter says in his first epistle: "Clothe yourselves, all of you, with humility toward one another, for God opposes the proud, but gives grace to the humble. Humble yourselves therefore under the mighty hand of God, that in due time he may exalt you" (1 Pt 5:5–6). Humility is an essential condition for receiving the fullness of the gifts of the Spirit. "For every one who exalts himself will be humbled, and he who humbles himself will be exalted," the Gospel says (Lk 14:11).

Humility has several aspects. It consists first of all in recognizing our faults. Repentance is very powerful in attracting the Holy Spirit. It is recognizing that we are nothing by ourselves, that everything is given to us. Everything we are and everything we accomplish is a free gift of God's mercy.

---

7. Thérèse of Lisieux, *St. Therese of Lisieux: Her Last Conversations*, trans. John Clarke, OCD (Washington, D.C.: ICS, 1977), July 11.6.

Being humble also means being reconciled to our own weakness, recognizing and accepting our limits. Remember these words of St. Thérèse of Lisieux, when speaking about pleasing God "in my little soul; what pleases Him is *that He sees me loving my littleness* and my *poverty.* . . . Ah! let us remain then *very far* from all that sparkles, let us love our littleness, let us love to feel nothing, then we shall be poor in spirit, and Jesus will come look for us, and *however far* we may be, He will transform us in flames of love."[8]

Humility in the end means to lower oneself out of love, like Jesus, who washed the feet of his disciples and said: "I am among you as one who serves" (Lk 22:27).

Humility involves an attitude of openness in our humanity. If I am humble, I accept advice, even reproaches; I allow myself to receive from others. Pride, on the contrary, is a closed attitude: I am self-sufficient, I am always right, I don't need anyone. In a relationship with God, this is even more the case: the more we recognize that we are nothing by ourselves and depend totally on the bounty of God, the more we are in a position to receive his grace.

Often our lack of humility prevents God from filling us with graces as much as he would like. Consider what

8. Thérèse of Lisieux, *Letters, Vol. II*, LT 197.

Catherine Mectilde de Bar, a seventeenth-century French religious, wrote to her sisters:

> God asks for nothing more than to fill us with himself and his graces, but he sees us so full of pride and esteem for ourselves that it stops him from communicating with us. For if a soul is not rooted in true humility, it is unable to receive the gifts of God. Its self-love devours it, and God is obliged to leave it in its poverty, in its shadows and sterility, remaining in its nothingness, so much is an attitude of humility necessary.[9]

Let us rejoice then that all progress in humility, everything that lowers us and humbles us, exteriorly or interiorly, opens us more to the gifts of the Spirit and makes us more capable of receiving them.

4. Obedience

"And we are witnesses to these things, and so is the Holy Spirit whom God has given to those who obey him," the Acts of the Apostles says (5:32). It's clear that the more we desire to do God's will, the more we receive the grace

---

9. Catherine de Bar, *Adorer et Adhérer* (Paris: Éditions du Cerf, 1994), p. 113.

to do it. God gives his Spirit to those who are resolute in obeying him. God refuses nothing to those who refuse him nothing.

This obedience, which of course must not come from fear but be inspired by trust and love, is therefore an important form of spiritual receptivity.

It can come in different forms: obedience to the Word, to our superiors in the Church, or to legitimate human authority. It also is expressed by submission to one another in love, something that Paul insisted so much upon: "Be subject to one another out of reverence for Christ" (Eph 5:21). Each time we renounce our own will, freely and out of love for someone, we open ourselves to the grace of the Spirit.

Internal obedience to the movements and inspirations of the Spirit is another kind of Christian filial obedience. Faithfulness to one grace attracts other graces. Each time we obey a divine inspiration, our heart grows and becomes capable of receiving more.

I want also to insist upon something that might be called *obedience to life's events*. This doesn't involve falling into fatalism or passivity but welcoming in trust the situations we encounter, in the certainty that the Providence of the Father will arrange everything for our good.

This kind of obedience is centrally important. The more I accept the events of my life with confidence, the more I receive the grace of the Holy Spirit. God doesn't permit something to happen without at the same time granting us the necessary grace to live it out in a positive way. In accepting it, I am welcoming the grace that comes with it. Consenting to all the various aspects of life is a fundamental receptivity to the Spirit. Life takes on coherence and beauty when we accept it in its entirety.

Etty Hillesum writes:

This sort of feeling has been growing much stronger in me: a hint of eternity steals through my smallest daily activities and perceptions. I am not alone in my tiredness or sickness or fears, but at one with millions of others from many centuries, and it is all part of life, and yet life is beautiful and meaningful too. It is meaningful even in its meaninglessness, provided one makes room in one's life for everything, and accepts life as one indivisible whole, for then one becomes whole in oneself. But as soon as one tries to exclude certain parts of life, refusing to accept them and arrogantly opting for this and not that part of life, yes, then it does become meaningless because it is no longer a whole, and everything then becomes quite arbitrary.[10]

Jesus refers to this form of obedience when speaking to Peter during his apparition on the shore of Lake Galilee after the Resurrection: "Truly, truly, I say to you, when you were young, you girded yourself and walked where you would; but when you are old, you will stretch out your hands, and another will gird you and carry you where you do not wish to go" (Jn 21:18).

These words apply to the martyrdom of Peter, but we can also understand them in a much more general way. Life sometimes leads us down paths we haven't chosen but which we must consent to out of love. This consent then becomes a source of grace, a way of union with God, and an experience of the presence of the Holy Spirit, who comes to the aid of our weakness. In his first epistle, Peter expresses it this way: "But rejoice in so far as you share Christ's sufferings, that you may also rejoice and be glad when his glory is revealed. If you are reproached for the name of Christ, you are blessed, because the spirit of glory and of God rests upon you" (1 Pt 4: 13–14). We

---

10. Etty Hillesum, *Etty: The Letters and Diaries of Etty Hillesum, 1941–1943*, ed. Klaas A. D. Smelik, trans. Arnold J. Pomerans (Grand Rapids, Mich.: William B. Eerdmans, 2002), p. 466.

can understand these words very broadly: each time we accept the conflicts and difficulties of life with faith in Christ and for love of him, the Holy Spirit rests upon us.

5. Practice of Interior Peace

If we want to be open to the grace of the Holy Spirit, we must struggle, insofar as it depends on us, to preserve our interior peace. "Strive to preserve your heart in peace; let no event of this world disturb it; reflect that all must come to an end. Take neither great nor little notice of who is with or against you, and try always to please God."[11]

"I have calmed and quieted my soul," says the Psalms (131:2). The more our hearts are peaceful and untroubled, the more they can receive the movement, light, and help of the Holy Spirit. On the contrary, worry, agitation, and anxiety close us off from grace.

"In returning and rest you shall be saved; in quietness and in trust shall be your strength," says the prophet Isaiah (Is 30:15).

Keep this in mind: only when we are in a state of peace do we have good discernment, see clearly in the various situations that confront us, and find the right

---

11. John of the Cross, *Sayings of Light and Love*, 154–155 in *The Collected Works of St. John of the Cross*, p. 55.

remedies for our problems. Tempestuous times, periods of trouble and worry, are bound to come, but our perception of reality is so distorted by negative emotions that we must wait for peace to return before changing any fundamental resolutions.

Mectilde de Bar counseled one of her sisters: "Be faithful in keeping your interior peace, because, once we've lost it, we don't see a thing, we don't know where we're going!"[12]

6. Live in the Present Moment

Another important condition for receiving the Holy Spirit is to live in the present moment. The more we are in the present—neither looking back nor anticipating what is to come—the more we are in touch with the real, with God, with interior resources that empower us to face up to living in the here and now—the more receptive we are to the work of grace. Sterile regrets, rumination on the past, and worries about the future cut us off from divine grace. If we entrust the past to the mercy of God and trust the future to his providence, doing just what is required

---

12. Catherine de Bar, à l'écoute de saint Benoît (Rouen: Bénédictines du Saint-Sacrement, 1979), p. 65.

of us today, so much the more we dispose ourselves to receive the grace we need day by day.

7. Detachment

Flexibility and detachment are necessary parts of letting the Spirit act in us by keeping our hearts free and clear from everything. If we are too attached to our plans, our way of seeing things, our own wisdom, we do not leave a place for the Spirit. I heard Sister Elvira, the founder of Cenacle (a wonderful charitable group that helps young drug addicts), say during a conference for priests: "I am always ready five minutes from now to do the exact opposite of what I had planned!"

Of course, we must have plans and undertake projects—but with total detachment. "Your heart must not be enslaved by anything. When you form some desire, it should not be such as to cause you pain in case of failure, but you should keep your spirit as tranquil as though you had never wished for anything," said Juan de Bonilla, a seventeenth-century Franciscan spiritual writer.[13] This detachment opens us wide to the Spirit's movements.

---

13. Juan de Bonilla as quoted in Jacques Philippe, *Searching for and Maintaining Peace: A Small Treatise on Peace of Heart*, trans. George and Jannie Driscoll (Staten Island, N.Y.: Society of St. Paul, 2002). Kindle version.

8. Gratitude

Gratitude is another very powerful attitude for attracting the grace of the Holy Spirit. Thérèse of Lisieux offers this testimonial to it:

> It is the spirit of gratitude which draws down upon us the overflow of God's grace . . . for no sooner have we thanked Him for one blessing than He hastens to send us ten additional favors in return. Then, when we show our gratitude for these new gifts, He multiplies His benedictions to such a degree that there seems to be a constant stream of divine grace ever coming our way. . . . This has been my own personal experience; try it out for yourself and see. For all that Our Lord is constantly giving me, my gratitude is boundless, and I try to prove it to Him in a thousand different ways.[14]

Under its light and humorous surface, this text contains a very profound truth: gratitude opens us up to the gifts of grace. Not that it makes God more generous (for he is fully so), but it makes us more open and receptive to his love, it distracts us from ourselves in

---

14. Geneviève of the Holy Face (Céline Martin), *My Sister Saint Thérèse* (Charlotte, N.C.: TAN Books, 1997), Chapter IV. E-book.

order to turn us entirely toward him. Gratitude is very fruitful because it is a sign that we have really understood and welcomed the love of God, and it puts us in a position to receive even more. "For to him who has will more be given, and he will have abundance; but from him who has not [who doesn't realize what he's already received], even what he has will be taken away," Jesus says (Mt 13:12).

Love is drawn to love. Gratitude is an extremely efficacious attitude of receptivity, while ingratitude, complaint, jealousy, and defensiveness close our hearts and deprive us of God's gifts. St. Bernard expresses this in a commentary on the gospel story of the lepers: all were healed by Jesus, but only one, a Samaritan, came back to give him thanks:

> Happy is the one who returns each gift of grace to him in whom is the fullness of all grace. So long as we do not betray ourselves as ungrateful to God for what we have received, we make a space for grace within us so that we merit to receive still more. Surely our ingratitude alone impedes us from progress in our conversion, since the giver, supposes that what he gives is in a sense lost if it is received ungratefully; so he is cautious about giving more, lest the more he confers to the ingrate, the more he loses. Hence he who considers

himself to be a foreigner is happy, for he responds even to small kindnesses with large gratitude.[15]

Consider also the similar words of Mectilde de Bar: "I beg of you, my child, to spend all your life in love of humble acknowledgment, in thanking God, in praising him and blessing him for all his blessings. It is a holy practice and one which has led me to growth in graces and to marvels without equal. In thanking Our Lord, you draw to yourself new blessings."[16]

Conclusion

If we try day by day to act as I have described, we will surely be open to the Spirit, and he can work in us. This doesn't mean we will always feel his presence and his action, for those things are sometimes hidden, as I have pointed out, but the fruits will come little by little. This is not a matter of doing everything said here perfectly but of persevering with good will and without discouragement in this direction.

---

15. Bernard of Clairvaux, *Bernard of Clairvaux: Monastic Sermons* (Collegeville, Minn.: Liturgical Press, 2016), pp. 157–158.

16. J. Daoust, *Le message eucharistique de Mère Mectilde du Saint Sacrement* (Paris: Téqui, 1979), p. 69.

Two last remarks.

First, the manner of behaving I have described is characteristic of Mary. This can easily be shown. The Virgin never ceased practicing in a perfect way each one of these points: prayer, trust, humility, obedience, peace, detachment, living in the present moment, and gratitude. The ultimate secret for receiving the abundance of the Spirit is to trust ourselves totally to the Holy Virgin, so that she will teach us her interior disposition, keep us faithful every day of our lives, and pray for what we are lacking. The closer we are to Mary, the more we receive the Holy Spirit.

Second, each of the attitudes I have mentioned expresses *the spirit of faith*.

Prayer is obviously an act of faith. *Trust* is also derived from faith. *Humility* (acceptance of my littleness) is an act of faith: I can accept myself in my littleness because I place all my faith in God and hope for everything from his mercy. *Obedience* is also an expression of faith in the goodness of God and his faithfulness. *Peace* is founded on faith: how can we be at peace in an uncertain world, if not because we put all our faith in the victory of Christ? *Living in the present moment* is also an act of faith: I give back to God my past and my future, and I believe that he is with me today. *Detachment* is an act of faith in the same way: I can be free and detached while facing everything in this world because I know that God's love is the essential good that will never fail me. As for *gratitude*, it is also an expression of faith in the bounty and the faithfulness of the Lord.

These two closing remarks are really only one: the greatness of Mary is the greatness of her faith. She was filled with the Spirit because of her faith, and the thing she most desires to communicate to us is precisely the force of her faith.

It is by faith that every grace, every gift of the Spirit, every divine blessing comes to us, as St. Paul ceaselessly affirms. Faith is the essence of our capacity to receive the free gift of God. And here we see why Jesus insists so much on this point in the Gospel: "Where is your faith?" (Lk 8:25).

CHAPTER 2

Living in God's Sight
with Thérèse of Lisieux

For Thérèse of the Child Jesus, the glance is very important. Anything can be said and communicated in a simple exchange of glances. A mutual look is the deepest and richest communion we can have, on earth, but it will especially be the case in the Kingdom. This exchange of loving glances between Thérèse and Jesus was the heart of her contemplative life. "I need the glance of my Divine Savior," she wrote.[1] The glance of Jesus was a space in which Thérèse absolutely needed to live, to be herself, to be free. She needed it so as not to be imprisoned by the looks of others or by her own looking in on herself, as we'll see later. Jesus' glance is not one that's judgmental, an accusing, enclosing stare, but

---

1. Thérèse of Lisieux, *The Poetry of Saint Thérèse of Lisieux*, trans. Donald Kinney, OCD (Washington, D.C.: ICS Publications, 1995), PN 32.

a glance that liberates and is encouraging, a look of compassion and mercy.

Never Stray from Jesus' Sight

Thérèse was seven when she saw the ocean for the first time at Trouville. It made a deep impression on her. Watching a little sailboat, she recalled, she "made the resolution never to wander far away from the glance of Jesus in order to travel peacefully toward the eternal shore!"[2]

There are, of course, different aspects to the divine glance. It is the look of the Creator on his creature by which he makes it live. It is the tender glance of the Father on his child. For Thérèse, who felt called to the religious life, it was the glance of Jesus the bridegroom on his spouse. The glance of Jesus is life-giving. It is a glance that chooses, that distinguishes in order to select. This is the mystery of vocation.

St. Thérèse often expressed surprise at the free choice of God in her life. God does not call those who are worthy but those who please him, out of pure mercy, and

---

2. Thérèse of Lisieux, *Story of a Soul: The Autobiography of St. Thérèse of Lisieux*, trans. John Clarke, OCD (Washington, D.C.: ICS Publications, 1996), p. 50. Kindle edition.

she desired to take refuge in the grace of God's merciful choice for her.

God's glance is also one that adorns with beauty. Thérèse took from St. John of the Cross the idea that merely by his glance, God clothes his creatures in beauty. St. John wrote:

Scattering a thousand graces,

He passed through these groves in haste,

And, looking upon them as he went,

Left them, by his glance alone,

clothed with beauty.[3]

God's glance imprints a resemblance with Jesus. And it gives life and fruitfulness. This glance receives the other in his poverty. It is a glance of understanding.

At the time of her First Communion, Thérèse wrote, Jesus and she had been looking at each other a long time and they understood each other. "That day, it was no longer simply a look, it was a fusion; they were no longer two, Thérèse had vanished as a drop of water is lost in the immensity of the ocean."[4]

---

3. John of the Cross, *Spiritual Canticle*, 5, in John of the Cross, *The Spiritual Canticle & Poems*, trans. E. Allison Peers (New York: Burns & Oates, 1978), p. 26.

4. Therese of Lisieux, *Story of a Soul*, p. 77.

God's glance is a look that purifies, "like the fire that transforms everything into itself," as Thérèse once wrote.[5] And so also it rejuvenates. Here is a truth worth meditating on: we are purified by allowing God to look on us, placing ourselves in his loving glance. Why is this so?

First of all, it is because our holiness comes from God as a participation in his divine holiness. St. Thérèse goes so far as tell God, "I desire, in a word, to be a Saint, but I feel my helplessness and I beg you, O my God! to be yourself my Sanctity!"[6]

When God looks at us, however, he sees us through his Son, through whose merit we have obtained forgiveness of our sins. Because of his Son and his offering on the Cross, God forgives us and purifies us of our sins.

The worst impurity is not letting ourselves be looked upon by God, fleeing from his glance, lacking trust in his love and hope for his mercy.

In this era of self-absorption and 'selfies,' we spend much time looking at ourselves (with approval or disappointment, as the case may be), obsessed with our image instead of looking at God and letting ourselves be seen by

---

5. Thérèse of Lisieux, "Prayer 6: Act of Oblation to Merciful Love," *The Prayers of Saint Thérèse of Lisieux: The Act of Oblation*, trans. Aletheia Kane, OCD (Washington, D.C.: ICS, 1997), p. 54.

6. Thérèse of Lisieux, *The Prayers of Saint Thérèse of Lisieux*, p. 54.

him. How impure is this narcissistic attitude of constant focus on self! We focus on ourselves instead of making God the center of our lives.

In addition, Jesus' glance purifies because it is a look of hope. Jesus doesn't consider our poverty, our woundedness, our human blemishes; he sees the children of God in us, the glory and splendor already ours. He knows our human deficiencies are temporary and his grace will bring us to fulfillment one day, provided we believe in his love and expose ourselves to it. "We shall all be changed, in a moment, in the twinkling of an eye," St. Paul says (1 Cor 15:51–52). God sees us already in glory and rejoices in our future beauty, which for him is the present. Thérèse one day asked herself how the Good Lord who loves us so much could bear to see us suffer here below. Her response: "already God sees us in glory. He takes delight in our eternal beatitude!"[7]

In a commentary on the gospel of St. Matthew's calling (Mt 9:9–13), Pope Francis spoke of the power that Jesus' gaze has to transform a person.

> Jesus stopped; he did not quickly turn away. He looked at Matthew calmly, peacefully. He looked at

---

7. Thérèse of Lisieux, *Letters of St. Thérèse of Lisieux, Volume I: 1877–1890*, trans. John Clarke, OCD (Washington, D.C.: ICS, 1982), p. 629. Kindle edition.

him with eyes of mercy; he looked at him as no one
had ever looked at him before. And that look unlocked
Matthew's heart; it set him free, it healed him, it gave
him hope, a new life. . . . This is our story, and it is
like that of so many others. Each of us can say: "I, too,
am a sinner, whom Jesus has looked upon."[8]

To let Jesus look at us: it is the most important thing in
our life.

The Veiled Glance of Jesus

St. Thérèse spoke of another important aspect to the
divine glance: the veiled glance of Jesus in his Passion. She
was deeply affected by the image of the suffering servant
in Isaiah and by the mystery of the Holy Face without
beauty or *radiance*. Calling these words "the foundation
of my whole piety," she said: "I also have desired to be
without beauty, to tread the winepress alone, unknown
by every creature."[9]

In the Holy Face she contemplates the revelation of
Jesus' infinite love: the most dazzling of the children of

8. Francis, *The Infinite Tenderness of God* (Frederick, MD: The Word Among Us,
2016), p. 83.

9. Thérèse of Lisieux, *Her Last Conversations*, August 5.9.

men was disfigured, his beauty hidden, because he had taken upon himself all our stains and weaknesses, thus enabling us to regain our original beauty and, still more, to be clothed in divine glory.

In this she finds a call to welcome suffering and humiliation as a grace, a privilege; by their means we enter into an intimate communion with the heart of Jesus. The tears veiling Jesus' glance are an invitation to console him by accepting suffering with him.

It is also an invitation not to seek glory in the eyes of men but to be hidden with him. St. Thérèse said, "Your Face is my only wealth. I ask for nothing more. Hiding myself in it unceasingly, I will resemble you, Jesus."[10]

Look especially at how Thérèse considers the suffering of her father during his sickness, which was terribly humiliating for him and for the whole family. Due to a cerebral degeneration, Mr. Martin had to be admitted to Our Savior of Caen—a *crazy house*, as they said at the time—where he spent three years. This was a very painful trial for Thérèse, all the more so because the gossips of Lisieux didn't hesitate to say her poor father had lost his mind because all of his daughters entered religious life. Conscious at times of his condition, he accepted it,

---

10. Thérèse of Lisieux, *The Poetry of Saint Thérèse of Lisieux*, PN 20.

saying: "I never had any humiliations in my life, and I needed one."[11]

He who was such a faithful image of the Father now resembled the suffering Son. Thérèse considered this trial to be a gift, a choice by Jesus, which she described in a poem written to her father after his death:

> A glance from the Divine Face
> Came to test you by a glorious choice.[12]

This painful trial was an invitation to turn toward the source of all fatherhood, God's fatherhood that nothing can diminish.

The Soul's Need to Live in Jesus' Gaze

For all the reasons noted here, St. Thérèse had an intense need to remain constantly in God's gaze, writing:

> My God's glance, his ravishing Smile,
> That is Heaven for me![13]

She absolutely needed Jesus' gaze, so as not to focus inward toward herself but outward, toward others.

---

11. Thérèse of Lisieux, *Story of a Soul*, p. 543.

12. Thérèse of Lisieux, PN 8.

13. Thérèse of Lisieux, PN 32.

As we all realize, the gaze of others can be positive or negative.

Thérèse was grateful when the regard of another carried some blessing or encouragement: her father's gaze, full of tenderness; the gaze of her sisters who loved her and encouraged her; the regard of her superiors at Carmel who trusted her.

She also experienced the limits of another's regard. She was often judged poorly by some of her sisters at Carmel, who thought her slow and infantile. Most people had no idea of the depth of her spiritual life or her suffering.

One of her novices was afraid of her and avoided her. But she accepted misunderstanding and did not try to justify herself. She wanted to live hidden, seen not by creatures but by Jesus alone.

As for her self-gaze, Thérèse's view of herself gradually underwent a great change.

At the start of her life at Carmel, experiencing her limits, her weakness, her imperfections, she tended to become discouraged and anxious, fearing that the Lord wasn't happy with her. But having discovered the "little way," she came to understand better God's merciful, fatherly love, and she became freer. She retained her ardent desire to become holy, to please God, to respond to his love, but she realized that what she called her "smallness" was not an obstacle to sanctity; it was a grace. Her smallness obliged her to stop depending on herself and count only on God's mercy, abandon herself entirely to him, and love with limitless trust.

As a result, Thérèse no longer dwelt upon her limits and weakness. She was turned totally toward God with infinite trust and so was perfectly receptive of divine grace, working within her what she could not accomplish by her own strength and leading her to the summit of love.

In her writings, for example, Thérèse noted that she often fell asleep during silent prayer. Here, she remarked, was proof that she was "far from being a saint. . . . I remember that little children are as pleasing to their parents when they are asleep as well as when they are awake."[14]

What mattered for Thérèse was not what she did or didn't do but God's gaze on her, the loving look of a father on his little child. Instead of despairing, she rejoiced in that loving gaze.

Thérèse let herself be loved just as she was, without ever doubting that God's gaze on her was a gaze of love. That gave her a great capacity to accept herself—and so to

---

14. Thérèse of Lisieux, *Story of a Soul*, p. 165.

forget herself completely in order to be fully receptive to God's love and give all to others. Let us ask for the grace to live as Thérèse did, in God's sight, and to receive from his gaze the benefits mentioned here, reminding ourselves that at the heart of it lies an act of faith.

Sometimes we will experience this look of tenderness that makes us free, but sometimes we will feel nothing. Yet God's action is far more vast and deep than any sensory experience. Our part is to live in faith and, in this act of faith, embrace the divine gaze upon us, remaining in it trustingly.

Finally, let us ask ourselves how we look upon others. Does our gaze, like God's, give life, freedom, and encouragement; is it a look of hope? Or is it a look of judgment, condemnation, and constraint?

A simple look can give life, but it can also give death. Let us ask for the grace to see each person with the eyes of Jesus, so that our eyes communicate life and hope to those we encounter.

CHAPTER 3

"When I Am Weak, Then I Am Strong!"

One of the themes that Scripture proposes for our consideration is the paradox of strength in weakness. It is found especially in the writings of St. Paul. We draw strength from consenting to our weakness. This is neither easily understood nor easily practiced. It requires much trust in God and much humility. But, today especially, it is extremely important. Using the testimonies of St. Paul and other witnesses, particularly St. Thérèse of Lisieux, I turn to it now.

The Modern World Relegates Us to Our Weakness

There are several reasons why this image of humanity confronting its weakness is particularly timely now.

Contemporary Western society is creating people who are more and more fragile. The disintegration of the family and of social relationships, the hedonistic mentality centered on the quest for immediate satisfaction, the difficulty in transmitting solid human values from one generation to another, the loss of contact with nature—these are among the principal causes. At the same time, this world of ours is becoming more and more powerful from a technological point of view, in which the will to control all is pervasive. Paradoxically, yet perhaps providentially, in the face of this technological power, individual persons are increasingly compelled to confront their personal weaknesses. Demanding efficiency, the technological mentality gives rise to a demand for an invasiveness that enters into every aspect of life, forcing many people, sometimes cruelly, to face up to their limits and their vulnerabilities. It is required of every person that he or she be competent in everything and succeed in all areas—work, social life, leisure activities, sex, and more.

Technological invasiveness dehumanizes relationships and demeans people. Machines appear to be more intelligent and competent than men and women. Many people worry that robots will one day replace them in their work.

Another product of technology is an overabundance of information. Media infiltrate the most remote recesses of private life. On the pretext of giving information, newspapers, television, and social media churn out the misery and failing of humankind more than in any other era, catering to unhealthy tastes as they do so.

The Holy Spirit Wants a Church of the Poor

There is a second reason, of a wholly different order, why facing up to our weakness is inevitable. God wants to reduce human pride to nothing, especially now. The more the Church progresses through history, the more poor and humble a Church she must become, in order to be filled with the grace of the Holy Spirit and respond to it.

The Holy Spirit wants to fashion the Church according to the model of the Beatitudes (Mt 5:1–12), which are not based on human strength but on the strength of God. Not on human wisdom but the wisdom of the Cross. Here is a Church able to address every wound and every inadequacy with love. But for that to happen, pride and human ambition in all their forms must go.

Here are passages from Scripture that speak of God's intervention in the end times, the Day of the Lord, when the vanity of human pride will be made plain for all to see:

> The haughty looks of man shall be brought low . . . the Lord alone will be exalted in that day. (Is 2:11)

> On that day you shall not be put to shame because of the deeds by which you have rebelled against me; for then I will remove from your midst your proudly exultant ones, and you shall no longer be haughty in my holy mountain. For I will leave in the midst of you a people humble and lowly. They shall seek refuge in the name of the Lord. (Zep 3:11–12)

Similar language occurs when St. Paul speaks of those whom God chose to establish his Church at Corinth.

> For the foolishness of God is wiser than men, and the weakness of God is stronger than men. For consider your call, brethren; not many of you were wise according to worldly standards, not many were powerful, not many were of noble birth; but God chose what is foolish in the world to shame the wise, God chose what is weak in the world to shame the strong, God chose what is low and despised in the world, even things that are not, to bring to nothing things that

are, so that no human being might boast in the presence of God. (1 Cor 1:25–29)

God does not seek to humiliate or destroy mankind. On the contrary, he wishes to glorify humanity beyond anything we can imagine and to confer on us a sovereign grandeur. "No eye has seen, nor ear heard, nor the heart of man conceived, what God has prepared for those who love him" (1 Cor 2:9).

But to make this exultation possible, to receive the fullness of God's salvation, to allow the grace of the Holy Spirit to act, we must confront our radical poverty. We must grasp the fact that God's gifts are absolutely free and beyond our power to acquire on our own. They are the fruit of God's mercy, not human merit.

Only humility, poverty of spirit, makes us capable of receiving the rich gifts God wants to give us in order to exalt us in his glory. Without a poor and humble heart, we seek to snatch God's gifts for our benefit—and the result is to nourish spiritual pride rather than placing them at the service of others. God's salvation is a work of pure mercy, as St. Paul points out in the Letter to the Romans:

For he says to Moses, "I will have mercy on whom I have mercy, and I will have compassion on whom I have compassion." So it depends not upon man's will or exertion, but upon God's mercy. (Rom 9:15–16)

The More I Want to Be Holy, the More Aware I Become of My Powerlessness

The more we advance in holiness, St. Thérèse said, the more aware we become of our radical weakness. Although asceticism is necessary for the spiritual life, we must realize that in a certain sense all asceticism is destined to fail. Human beings cannot change themselves by their own power.

We must desire holiness and do all we can to acquire it. Thérèse said: "I don't want to be a saint by halves!"[1] But the more that we drive ourselves to attain it, the more we realize that it exceeds our human capacity. When a ray of sunlight cuts through a dark room, we see that the air is filled with many more dust particles than we could have imagined. Just so, the closer the soul is to God, the more it sees its own poverty—its hardness of heart, its faults and blemishes.

Testifying in her autobiography to her awareness that she stood in relation to the saints as a grain of sand

---

1. Thérèse of Lisieux, *The Story of a Soul*, p. 27.

to majestic mountains—and yet she also wanted to be a saint!—Thérèse concluded that she must not become discouraged, that holiness was possible for her because God had given her this desire and that he is just and faithful. "I wanted to find an elevator which would raise me to Jesus, for I am too small to climb the rough stairway of perfection."[2] After searching the Scriptures, she decided that she must let God act, and for that, she must remain little and become ever more so.

We can't transform ourselves or effect our own conversion: only God's grace can reach the extremity of our weakness. In faithfulness to the gospel—and also so that we don't weigh down others with a burden we can't carry ourselves—we must understand that Christianity is not a religion of human efforts but of grace. That doesn't mean we should do nothing, but we should see our efforts in context. We strive not to exercise human power but to open ourselves to grace. And an essential condition for opening ourselves to the grace of the Holy Spirit is to be free of all forms of pride, so as to become little and humble before God. "But this is the man to whom I will look, he that is humble and contrite in spirit, and trembles at my word" (Is 66:2).

---

2. Thérèse of Lisieux, *The Story of a Soul*, p. 207.

From Human Poverty to Spiritual Poverty

There is a text by a Carthusian monk that underlines the need to face up to human weakness, especially in a setting like a monastery completely animated by the quest for God, as the Carthusian monastery can be. The disconcerting experience of human poverty, our own and that of others, can lead little by little to true poverty of spirit.

The "habitual shortcomings of human nature" he writes, are as present in the monastery as anywhere else. But that is a necessary part of the process of self-examination and growth in self-understanding. "We first discover mediocrity in others and afterwards, in ourselves."[3] And as we do, our self-absorption fades in the light of the risen Christ. This is the way the monk must follow: "He must learn never to focus on himself but to be taken up in the movement of a divine love."[4]

Poverty of spirit, the first of the Beatitudes, is the gateway to the Kingdom of Heaven (Mt 5:3). Spiritual poverty is the freedom to receive freely and give everything freely, a freedom possible only by the death of all self-love, all concentration on self. Then we are turned

---

3. The Carthusian Order in England, *The Wound of Love: A Carthusian Miscellany*, (Herefordshire: Gracewing, 2006), p. 33.

4. The Carthusian Order in England, *The Wound of Love*, p. 34.

entirely toward God to receive without measure and toward others to give without keeping score.

Paul's Experience

The theme of humankind confronted with its weakness is in the foreground of St. Paul's works, especially in the Second Letter to the Corinthians when he speaks of his mysterious "thorn in the flesh":

> If I must boast, I will boast of the things that show my weakness. . . . A thorn was given me in the flesh, a messenger of Satan, to harass me, to keep me from being too elated. Three times I besought the Lord about this, that it should leave me; but he said to me, "My grace is sufficient for you, for my power is made perfect in weakness." I will all the more gladly boast of my weaknesses, that the power of Christ may rest upon me. For the sake of Christ, then, I am content with weaknesses, insults, hardships, persecutions, and calamities; for when I am weak, then I am strong. (2 Cor 11:30, 12:7–10)

What is this thorn in the flesh? We don't know. It is some condition or suffering, ever present and humiliating, from which Paul would have preferred to be free, thinking it an obstacle to the fruitfulness of his mission. But the Lord made him understand that, on the contrary, it was best that he continue to have this weakness: God's power is "made perfect in weakness" (2 Cor 12:9).

Paul can say his strength is in weakness because when he is realistic about the weakness, he is obliged to place himself totally in Christ's hands by an act of faith; and, that done, his human capacities no longer work in him, but the grace of Christ. "It is no longer I who live, but Christ who lives in me" (Gal 2:20).

The experience of radical weakness compels us to a kind of surrender by which we recognize our poverty, accept the fact that we are not absolute masters of our lives, count on God alone, and place ourselves at his mercy with boundless trust. Then God acts and does splendid things, things sometimes visible but often hidden.

Speaking in the Second Letter to the Corinthians of a painful trial he had undergone (we don't know exactly what), Paul says this: "We were so utterly, unbearably crushed that we despaired of life itself. Why, we felt that we had received the sentence of death; but that was to make us rely not on ourselves but on God who raises the dead" (2 Cor 1:8–9).

The outcome of this trial, with its radical experience of weakness, was positive since it led Paul to put away confidence in himself in favor of confidence in God and God's power over life. Thanks to faith, human weakness becomes an opening for God's strength.

Faith, Opening Mankind's Weakness to the Power of God

Paul has a well-developed understanding of the beauty of apostolic ministry and its glory. Having spoken of this glory, greater than the ministry of Moses, he says:

> But we have this treasure in earthen vessels, to show that the transcendent power belongs to God and not to us. We are afflicted in every way, but not crushed; perplexed, but not driven to despair; persecuted, but not forsaken; struck down, but not destroyed; always carrying in the body the death of Jesus, so that the life of Jesus may also be manifested in our bodies. For while we live we are always being given up to death for Jesus' sake, so that the life of Jesus may be manifested in our mortal flesh.
>
> So death is at work in us, but life in you. . . . And so we speak, knowing that he who raised the Lord Jesus will raise us also with Jesus and bring us with you into his presence. (2 Cor 4:7–14)

I believe this passage is the most precise description we have of life as Christ's apostle, always at the limit of our forces, yet animated by a "spirit of faith" leading us to proclaim the message of the Gospel.

Weakness, Not an Obstacle but a Path

And so fragility and weakness aren't obstacles to holiness but the path to it. As Marie Eugène of the Child Jesus said, "If this poverty didn't exist, it would be necessary to create it as a support for our ascent to God."[5] The experience of weakness is positive because it effects a purification of faith, so that little by little it is founded only on God, on his Word and his promises, not on the self or other human entities. We learn to throw ourselves into God's arms in total confidence, in faith, counting on him to support us in his mercy and fidelity.

Rejoicing in Her Weaknesses

We find the same thought in St. Thérèse of Lisieux. In a letter to her cousin, Marie Guérin, she spoke of her

---

5. Marie-Eugène de l'Enfant-Jésus, quoted in Joël Guibert, *Renaître d'en haut: Une vie renouvelée par l'Esprit Saint* (Paris: Éditions de l'Emmanuel, 2008), p. 150.

extreme weakness, adding that by it, Jesus was teaching her "the science of rejoicing in her infirmities. . . . When we see ourselves as so miserable, then we no longer wish to consider ourselves, and we look only on the unique Beloved!"[6]

In a letter to her sister and godmother, Marie of the Sacred Heart, Thérèse expressed a magnificent hope: that when we have become truly poor in spirit "Jesus will come to look for us, and *however far* we may be, He will transform us in flames of love."[7] Humility attracts the fire of the Holy Spirit.

Love Is a Victory of Weakness

As I have already said, the experience of weakness purifies faith and hope so that they come to be founded only on God—faith on his word, hope on his limitless mercy.

Our love of neighbor is purified, too. The experience of weakness leads us to stop judging others, treating them with gentleness, humility, and understanding instead. Our relationship with God is intensified: seeing ourselves so poor, we are obliged to invoke him constantly; putting

---

6. Thérèse of Lisieux, *Letters, Vol. II*, LT 109.

7. Thérèse of Lisieux, *Letters, Vol. II*, LT 197.

away self-love and turning ourselves totally to him. Our happiness is not in ourselves but in him.

The great mystery lying behind the positive face of human weakness is the mystery of love. In love there is a great power, but it is veiled in a mystery of weakness. Paul can say the weakness of God is stronger than human wisdom because God's weakness expresses his limitless love for humankind, whose human condition he wanted to take upon himself.

At the heart of all authentic love there is a mystery of weakness. Love means accepting and being accepted, as another Carthusian monk said, "without being judged or condemned, and without invidious comparisons. . . . Once we really begin to believe in the infinite tenderness of the Father, we are, as it were, obliged to descend ever more fully and joyfully into a realm in which we neither possess nor understand nor control anything."[8]

This weakness is not laziness or cowardice, not a devaluing of human efforts. Human enterprise is beautiful and necessary, not as a condition for meriting grace— it is given freely—but as an expression of good will, of our desire to respond fully to God's love. Human capacities

---

8. The Carthusian Order in England, p. 87.

and talents are not to be despised but developed—the Gospel makes this clear.

God will not save us without our collaboration. His love is freely given but can't be fully accepted without our choosing to do that. So there is a place for human effort. But it must be in its place. This isn't fretful or prideful perfectionism but doing what's asked of us day by day with simplicity, gentleness, peace, humility and trust, supported by God and not relying on ourselves, never worried or discouraged at reaching our limits but accepting them humbly and peacefully. St. Thérèse said: "We experience such great peace when we're totally poor, when we depend upon no one except God."[9]

Mary, Mother of the Poor and the Little Ones

The path of recognition and acceptance of weakness isn't always easy. It collides with pride, fear of not being accepted by others, and lack of trust in God. It demands a radical revolution that doesn't come easily to us: no longer thinking about ourselves but staying purely centered on God.

It helps a great deal to be close to the Virgin Mary. Thérèse expresses this in her last poem: "Near you,

---

9. Thérèse of Lisieux, *Her Last Conversations*, August 6.4.

Mary, I like to stay little."[10] Close to Mary, our weakness becomes lovable to us for we see God as our only true wealth. Mary's maternal tenderness offers us marvelous encouragement on this path of humility and love that she herself followed. In a homily at Lourdes on September 15, 2008, Pope Benedict XVI rejected the idea that this is "pious infantilism," declaring instead that "those who have attained the highest degree of spiritual maturity . . . know precisely how to acknowledge their weakness and their poverty before God."[11]

10. Thérèse of Lisieux, *The Poetry of St. Therese of Lisieux*, PN 54.

11. Benedict XVI, *Homily to France on the Occasion of the 150th Anniversary of the Apparitions of the Blessed Virgin Mary at Lourdes*, 15 September 2008, *www.vatican.va*.

CHAPTER 4

True and False Freedom

I f there is one thing we all desire, it is freedom. Yet this concept and its concrete manifestations are objects of a great deal of misunderstanding and painful disillusion. What is freedom? How do we achieve it? These questions are of vital importance.

First, I would like to offer some reflections on freedom in modern culture. Then, in the light of Christian revelation, thoughts on true freedom and how to achieve it.

The Idea of Freedom

The thirst for freedom has strongly affected Western culture for centuries. Western societies have changed greatly during this time in regard to individual liberties.

The Christian message is a message of freedom: "The truth will make you free" (Jn 8:32). Many passages in Scripture speak of the freedom God wishes to bestow on mankind.

Thus there seems to be a happy convergence between the aspirations of modern culture and the message of the gospel. In practice, though, things are not that simple. The freedom proposed by the gospel and the vision of freedom today do not always coincide. Some people even consider Christianity, or religion in general, to be freedom's worst enemy.

This is the great lie of modern atheism: to restore mankind to its freedom, it is necessary to do away with the idea of God. In reality, just the reverse is true: God is source and Redeemer of our freedom. The more attached we are to God, the more free we become. The further we are from him, the more at risk is our freedom.

There is a paradox here that requires our consideration. Although human liberty has made much progress over the centuries, people today do not feel as free as one might expect.

Human beings today appear to have more free space available to them than their forefathers did. Technology confers on us more power to act on our surroundings. We are much freer to choose our own religion and our beliefs—or disbeliefs (there will be no inquiry by the Inquisition). Individual freedoms are generally better guaranteed in Western societies (freedom of opinion, of conscience, of expression). Social conventions and family ties are less binding. We can marry without seeking anyone's permission. The parameters of acceptable conduct are much broader than before.

And yet, if modern man seems objectively more "free" than in other periods of history, there is nonetheless a subjective feeling that freedom is lacking. The demand for freedom, which marks the evolution of Western culture from the eighteenth century on, does not seem to have been satisfied. Consider some examples.

Thanks to the social sciences, people today are more conscious than people used to be of the social and psychological conditioning that can limit freedom and the influence of the subconscious on decisions. The result often is a tendency not to consider oneself truly responsible for one's actions and choices. Ultimately, one doubts the very existence of real freedom, while love sometimes is explained as a product of hormones more than free choice.

Frequently, too, people feel stifled living lives that fail to satisfy their deepest aspirations. More common than ever before is the flight from reality, the quest for distractions, the need to escape. That word—"escape"—occurs over and over in travel ads. Are we all in a prison that we need to escape?

Attitudes pointing to dissatisfaction with life and attempts to have a more intense or free way of life have never been more numerous, among them: taking drugs, seeking extreme sensations, drifting into dubious spiritual practices, resisting any kind of constraint or rules, claiming not to be bound by conventions, and exhibiting transgressive behavior.

It hardly seems we have really satisfied our thirst for freedom. Discovering and experiencing genuine freedom remain out of reach.

Here I want to describe four ways of understanding freedom that are present in our culture. No doubt there are others, but these appear to me the most important for us to examine. They can have positive aspects but negative ones as well.

Freedom and Omnipotence

Viewed from a "technical" perspective, freedom frequently is confused with power. The more we are capable of doing to transforming situations and reality, the more we are free.

This is partly true. We ought not to dismiss the progress that gives us more control over material, biological, social, and psychological reality, more know-how, and additional means of communicating. Very quickly, though, we come up against an obstacle: all technological power has its limits—there are always realities we can neither change nor master. Faced with situations in which we are weak or powerless, do we cease to be free? How free is freedom that fails whenever we encounter a situation in which we cannot be free? True freedom should be able to operate in every circumstance, including situations over which we lack control. Otherwise, it is not freedom.

Thus, a true notion of freedom should include a trusting acceptance of our limitations, our weaknesses and failures, and situations in which we are powerless because they are beyond our control. It must be able to exist alongside the weak and frail elements in every human life.

And this is possible. We aren't always free to change things, but we are always free to live through them in faith, hope, and love so that in every situation we grow humanly and spiritually. "In everything God works for good with those who love him" (Rom 8:28).

Freedom and Ability to Choose

There is a tendency to identify freedom with the ability to choose among a wide range of options: we are free in proportion to the number of choices we have. Today we want to be able to choose every aspect of our identity, even our sexuality (with the blessing of apologists for gender theory).

You might call this the "freedom supermarket." The bigger the store and the more products available, the freer we are. And it really is more pleasant to do one's shopping in a well-stocked supermarket rather than one of those depressing markets of Eastern Europe during the Communist era, with their limited variety of products and threadbare look. Yet this way of looking at things quickly comes to a dead end. The wide varieties of yogurt in the supermarket dairy case or the dozens of choices of flat screen televisions in the department store can give rise to anxiety in the end (which to choose?) or frustration (to choose one means rejecting others—and of course I *must* reject many simply because I can't afford them all). This overabundance of offerings hardly gives one a contented sense of freedom. Exhilarating at the start, it soon ends in disenchantment.

On a human level, choosing clearly means renouncing. If I marry a woman, I renounce all the others. Am I less free for that reason? As we pass through life, we make more decisions, and the number of choices available to us drops. Are we therefore less free? Freedom should grow with the years, not diminish!

Thinking of freedom this way can have harmful consequences. Today, on the pretext of keeping their freedom, many people do not get involved in anything or they indefinitely put off the time for decisive choices (like marriage). And the most rewarding things in life pass them by. Freedom has become its own negation—indecision— instead of what it should be: a capacity for being involved.

Facing various possibilities, it is good for us to choose among them. Yet perhaps the highest and most rewarding exercise of freedom is assenting to things we haven't chosen, welcoming in trust realities that transcend us.

Our real prison is ourselves: our limited perception of reality, our narrow-mindedness and narrow-heartedness. Experience often shows that we break out of this prison and open new horizons in accepting situations we haven't chosen and so come to perceive a deeper dimension of reality, more rich and more beautiful.

Human freedom is not so much a power to transform as a capacity to welcome. The most rewarding act of freedom ever made by a human being was the *fiat* of Mary, her trusting, loving "yes."

We notice, too, that the fundamental question is not whether we have more or less freedom of choice— freedom that in the end doesn't make much sense in isolation—but about the reasons that lead us to opt for one choice rather than another. What directs us to our decisions? A simple impulse, a desire? Or is it convention, the desire to do what everyone else does? Or even our fears, our faults, our defense mechanisms?

One of the paradoxes of modern life is how often people pretend to be free ("I'm a free man, a free woman," we hear so often on television) when in fact they are only following fashions or whims. Many people think of themselves as original while merely conforming to trends.

Let's ask ourselves the real question: What values guide and drive my freedom? Are they phantoms, illusions, or lies—or do they foster authentic fulfillment of my personality and my life?

If freedom is not directed toward a real good, driven by objective values, it simply ceases to exist. There is no freedom except in relation to a truth that guides it and directs it. Only truth makes us free, as the Gospel of John says. Without truth, without reference points, without guiding principles, without "law," freedom becomes folly. There is no freedom without obedience to a truth greater than ourselves.

Freedom and Independence.

What about freedom as independence from anybody or anything else? Here, too, we finds a certain amount of truth. There is no freedom apart from a degree of autonomy that allows us to take a stance and make our choices without depending on others in a manner that keeps us from being ourselves. Sometimes we must cut loose from social constraints, confinements, draining relationships, or emotional entanglements in order to find true freedom.

That said, we can never do without others, never be absolutely self-sufficient. There is an illusory fantasy of self-sufficiency that comes from pride. We must accept our dependency on others for a lot of things; no one can achieve happiness and fulfillment in isolation from others. There is much, so very much, for which we need others.

True freedom isn't isolation but a capacity to engage with real people, to develop relationships, and to remain faithful to these alliances. An alliance with God, first, but also a whole ensemble of alliances with other human beings: family, various communities, religious family, and so on. Our very image of ourselves is constructed out of these relationships. There is no freedom without fidelity. Who is the most free? He or she who is faithful to the same person or community in spite of the hazards of life, the passage of time? Or the one who changes partners every year?

Winning our freedom doesn't mean emancipation from all dependency, from all ties. Rather, it brings the ability to discern between the ties that imprison us and those that build us up. It empowers us to avoid the dependencies that alienate us but also to welcome those that help us to be ourselves along with the true, loving relationships that help us discover ourselves—in particular, our radical dependence on God, from whom we receive everything. To be free means consenting to this dependency and learning to receive from others.

Freedom presupposes not being prisoners of habits, of social conformity. But this doesn't mean making a clean break with the past, inventing a new life from scratch as if nothing had preceded it. Scripture says, "Honor your father and your mother" (Ex 20:12)—in other words, recognize what you've received from those who went before you, despite their limits and imperfections; they have given you a history, a tradition. We must be original, creative, and inventive, but sensitive to what came before us, drawing our treasure, as Jesus says, from "what is new and what is old" (Mt 13:52).

Freedom and Spontaneity

To be free also signifies having the power to follow our impulses, realize our desires, follow our hearts, be freely ourselves, and affirm our personalities, not acting under constraints but doing what we want, acting as we see fit. These are currently trendy themes that advertising exploits very astutely to move us to buy particular products, services, or ideas regardless of whether they are really good for us.

Still, this view of things does have a bit of truth: someone whose life is fundamentally directed by what lies within him rather than by external constraints is free.

Sacred Scripture points in this direction. It is the magnificent promise of the New Covenant in Jeremiah: to be directed not by an exterior law written on stone tablets but by the law written on our hearts that directs us spontaneously to do what is good: "But this is the covenant which I will make with the house of Israel after those days, says the Lord: I will put my law within them, and I will write it upon their hearts" (Jer 31:33).

That is accomplished by the gift of the Holy Spirit, who bestows true freedom, freedom proceeding from the Spirit, not from the Law or from the "flesh"—our wounded nature—as St. Paul says. True spontaneity comes from allowing ourselves to be led by the Spirit, for there is a convergence between what the Spirit desires and our most authentic personality: "Where the Spirit of the Lord is, there is freedom" (2 Cor 3:17).

There is, however, an obvious danger in equating freedom with spontaneity. We can easily fall into thinking freedom means realizing all our desires, all our wishes, including the most dubious ones. Everyday experience provides many examples of how impulsively following our desires and fantasies leads to brutal disillusion, even sorrowful slavery. This way of thinking of freedom cheapens the long and patient work that teaches us through direct encounters with others, with reality, with objective truth, to discern among all our desires and impulses those we should follow because they proceed from what is authentic in us and from the presence of the Spirit. Other desires and impulses, we then see, should be set aside inasmuch as they arise from our psychological wounds—from the "flesh" in St. Paul's sense.

Genuine spontaneity—that is, the ability to live in a just and fruitful manner simply by letting ourselves be moved by an interior impulse—is not acquired overnight. It requires long, patient work on our part along with openness to the work of the Holy Spirit. In this it resembles the freedom and flexibility of professional skaters or dancers that come from many hours of hard work.

Today people dream of a "cool" freedom achieved at low cost without pain or effort. But true freedom is costly; it requires work and renunciation. Sometimes it must be won at the point of a sword: "If your hand or your foot causes you to sin, cut it off," Jesus says (Mt 18:8). We must show no mercy to whatever separates us from our freedom as God's children. There is no freedom for us unless we are detached from everything.

Freedom is a grace but also a requirement, a burden we might sometimes prefer to be rid of. We cannot have freedom without responsibility, risk, and moments of doubt, anguish, perplexity. Some free decisions can only have a painful birth.

So what work on ourselves needs doing? This is essentially a work of discernment to perceive the nature, meaning, and origin of the impulses that drive us and the voices that call to us from within. We must recognize the consequences of our psycho-emotive wounds (emotionally disproportionate reactions, lack of freedom, mistaken perceptions of reality, false views of others or ourselves that hold us prisoner). We must step back from emotions, perceptions, and desires born of our wounds. And, simultaneously, we must heed ourselves and let our deepest aspirations emerge—desires that correspond to our true identity, with the Father's will for us, calls that summon us toward our real good.

Spontaneity is an excellent thing, provided it does not spring from superficial psychological conditioning but from our most genuine self. "Love and do what you will," St. Augustine said;[1] but love is the fruit of a long work of purifying the heart and learning to listen to our interior calls.

The Indissoluble Link between Freedom and Love

How do we escape the obstacles just described? How do we achieve an understanding of freedom that is realistic and accessible, and that orients us progressively to the experience of real freedom? The answer is by understanding the relationship between freedom and love. In love we find the fulfillment of freedom—but on the condition that we know what is meant by "love."

There is no love without freedom. Love presupposes freedom. A relationship governed by coercion, fear, or giving in order to get may be grounded in many things but certainly not love. Love only exists between people who freely give of themselves to one another. This is why the Church has fought so hard for centuries to insist on the freedom of consent of spouses in

---

1. Augustine of Hippo as quoted in John Leinenweber, *Love One Another, My Friends: Saint Augustine's Homilies on the First Letter of John* (Eugene, Or.: Wipf & Stock, 1989), p. 73.

marriage. This is why God respects human freedom so much. He doesn't want slaves but sons and daughters. Freedom is infinitely precious because it is the necessary condition for love to exist.

A few years ago I was reading the beautiful spiritual journal of Blessed Dina Bélanger of Quebec when something struck me. She often had apparitions of Jesus in which he asked for prayers and sometimes for sacrifices or the acceptance of some suffering on behalf of one person or another. One time a demon came in the appearance of Jesus to ask something similar of her. But Dina saw an enormous difference between the requests of Jesus and those of the Adversary. Jesus respected her freedom, and he asked without demanding; but the demon operated by compulsion and feelings of guilt. With Jesus, she felt peace. With the demon, she felt turmoil.

Sometimes, though, we forget that what I am describing also works the other way around: **there is no true freedom without love.** It is good to be free—but what do I mean to do with my freedom? *Freedom, to Do What?* is the title of a book by George Bernanos. The fullness of freedom is achieved in the gift of self out of love, in a mystery of union with others.

If freedom isn't realized in a choice to love that desires the good of the other, it becomes self-destructive.

Here is the paradox of the gospel: those who want to save their lives will lose them, while those who accept losing their lives—giving themselves in love—will save their lives. What the gospel says applies to everyone, for it does no more than state the deep, secret laws of life, things "hidden since the foundation of the world," (Mt 13:35) but relevant to all.

The only way to experience freedom that lasts and grows more and more intense is to love more and more. St. Paul tells the Corinthians it is not he who places restrictions on them but their own closed hearts (2 Cor 6:12). That is to say the lack of freedom arises from not loving enough. Love brings freedom. The more pure and intense love is, the more expansive is freedom. A loving heart is never closed.

Such freedom can be acquired (unlike the freedom of omnipotence of which we sometimes dream), but that takes time. Moreover, it is a grace, a gift of God, a fruit of the Holy Spirit. But once we can truly love God with all our heart, love any man or woman, whoever he or she may be, and love ourselves—fully accept ourselves, that is—we then are truly free.

St. Paul tells us what use to make of our freedom: "For though I am free from all men, I have made myself a slave to all, that I might win the more (1 Cor 9:19). "For

you were called to freedom, brethren; only do not use
your freedom as an opportunity for the flesh, but through
love be servants of one another" (Gal 5:13).

Love Is Founded on Faith and Hope

To be free is to be able to love in all circumstances. Christian freedom is not omnipotence but the power to grow
in love in all situations. Such freedom is humble but real.
It is guaranteed to us by Christ. And it is important to
realize that it presupposes a foundation in faith and hope.

To love in every situation requires trust in God, trust
in life, faith and hope. Faith and hope are, we might say,
love's wings—without which it can't take flight. As soon
as faith or hope are diminished, love also suffers.

Thus the only way to win freedom is to grow in faith,
hope, and love.

We are, however, always free to believe, to hope, and
to love. Even in prison, even in the worst of situations, a
person can always make acts of faith and hope together
with decisions in favor of love in his or her own heart.
Within us we possess an inalienable space of freedom.

It makes us more and more free to grow in faith, hope,
and love. The theological virtues have an immense liberating value: Faith frees us from doubt, error, lies, blindness,

and nonsense. Hope frees us from fear, discouragement, worry, and guilt. Love frees us from egoism, avarice, turning in on ourselves, and a narrow, meaningless life without value or fruitfulness. It frees us from frustrations and bitterness.

The measure of our freedom is the measure of our faith, of our hope, of our love.

So the path toward freedom lies in putting in place all that increases our faith, hope, and love: our daily decisions in favor of trust and charity; the means at our disposal for increasing the theological virtues within us— prayer, contact with the Word of God, the sacraments of the Church, the support of other believers, and so on. Everything that makes up the Christian life in all its diversity has only one goal: to help us achieve the full freedom of being children of God.

Discerning the Objective Deficiencies of Our Freedom

In this growth process, it is important to detect and recognize failures in freedom. Our healing begins with the recognition that we are ill.

We are not free when we are governed by something other than love—by the "flesh" in St. Paul's sense: our wounded psyche. Let me give some examples of situations that can more or less govern our choices and attitudes and cause a lack of freedom. This is hardly an exhaustive list, but just those situations that come readily to mind.

Egotistical covetousness: We pretend to love, but in fact we want to possess, to appropriate the other person to ourselves in order to satisfy our egotistical interests.

Pride: We want to be part of an elite corps, give free rein to our egotism, and show others that we are the best.

Fear: Our decisions often arise from a need to protect ourselves, denial, flight, fear of others' opinions, fear of displeasing someone, fear of what people will say. Yes, we must be prudent, but we should not allow ourselves to be governed by fear or worry. Decisions inspired by fear are bad decisions, and fear of suffering can cause more problems than suffering itself.

Guilt: It is a good thing to feel guilty in the face of an evil we have actually committed coupled with the determination to correct it and repair the harm. But guilt can become excessive. We may even fear we haven't done enough to please God because we have a false image of him. Guilt can be rooted in psychological wounds rather than authentic love. A person may have a sense of being in debt—having to pay a price to merit being loved.

(Sometimes one encounters children who subconsciously hold themselves to blame for their parents' divorce, for instance.)

Emotional attachment: I am doing what I think I must so as not to lose the affection or esteem of someone I cling to, denying my own authentic personality.

False obligations: For various reasons—social convention, fear of not living up to others' expectations—we impose duties on ourselves that neither God nor truth requires of us: for example, believing we must always please others. This often leads to perfectionism: I must be absolutely perfect if others are to accept me and love me. Or it may lead to legalism: what a catastrophe if I break some rule! We are prisoners of the letter of the law instead of interpreting the law according to its spirit.

Subconscious quid pro quo: We devote ourselves to someone or to a cause—but with the hidden objective of receiving something in return.

Hate: We are compelled by the desire for vengeance, to "make them pay" for the wrong others did us. It is normal sometimes to feel resentment, anger, and aggressiveness, but these emotions shouldn't govern our decisions.

Reaction to suffering: We are motivated not by something sought for its own sake but in reaction to a situation or event that we have not "digested," so to speak. For example, I suffered in a disappointing romantic relationship: I'll never love anyone again! A priest hurt me: I'm against the whole Church. I automatically oppose whatever someone thinks or says, not for objective reasons, but because I'm angry at the pain he or she caused me.

Mimicry: I imagine I'm obliged to imitate the behavior of someone, or some group, out of emotional attachment or a need for recognition or acceptance within this group.

Discouragement: Having lost hope or self-confidence, we metaphorically or literally "shrug our shoulders" out of laziness or withdrawal.

Sometimes we see behaviors that look good but, being governed by things other than love, are in fact bad. An act of great generosity can conceal self-interest or fear. Unfailing obedience can conceal immaturity. Pious, edifying attitudes can be products of mimicry or a need for recognition. Some people are externally irreproachable but have no interior freedom. Harmful consequences result: rigidity, suffocation, interior tension, exhaustion, anger, frustration, rebellion.

Then we must ask God for the grace to discern our failures of freedom, entrust them to him, and, little by little, seek healing.

In this process of clarifying motives, faithfulness to silent prayer, times of meditation, and spiritual accompaniment are often most valuable in helping us see how we have failed to be free.

The Happiness of the Soul, Free Because It Loves

Achieving freedom is costly, slow work. By way of encouragement, I direct you to several books on this theme which present the works of spiritual writers who have expressed the happiness of the soul that feels free because it is governed exclusively by love.

Glenn E. Myers, *Seeking Spiritual Intimacy: Journeying Deeper with Medieval Women of Faith* (Downers Grove, Ill.: Inter-Varsity Press, 2011). Read about the Seven Manners of Holy Love defined by Beatrice of Nazareth, a Cistercian nun from the Middle Ages, on pp. 67–81.

John of the Cross, *Spiritual Canticle*, 19, as quoted in John of the Cross, *The Spiritual Canticle & Poems*, trans. E. Allison Peers (New York: Burns & Oates, 1978).

Faustina Kowalska, *Diary of Saint Maria Faustina Kowalska: Divine Mercy in My Soul* (Stockbridge, Mass.: Marian Press, 2014), no. 890.

CHAPTER 5

Interior Peace, a Spiritual Urgency

The Call to Be at Peace

"But according to his promise we wait for new heavens and a new earth in which righteousness dwells. Therefore, beloved, since you wait for these, be zealous to be found by him without spot or blemish, and at peace" (2 Pt 3:13–14).

At the conclusion of a passage evoking the coming of the Day of the Lord at the end of time using traditional imagery of the Apocalypse, it's remarkable that St. Peter calls on us to find ourselves "at peace" on this day. Not in anguish or fear, but at peace.

Of course, we need not speculate on the end of time. Only the Father knows the day and the hour. But it seems to me there is a fundamental lesson here for today: the more the Church and the world run toward its arrival, and the more creation cries out in the sorrow of giving birth, the more the Christian is called to be in peace. The more the world goes through crises, the more society is marked by tensions and insecurities, the more necessary it is to find true peace, to let ourselves go in the profound peace of Christ.

Therein lies spiritual urgency. The more the Church marches on through history, the more she is called to live each of the Beatitudes, but especially the seventh: "Blessed are the peacemakers, for they shall be called sons of God" (Mt 5:9).

So there is a very strong call to let ourselves find peace in Christ, to welcome God's peace in our hearts. I would go as far as to say that the first duty of a Christian isn't to be perfect or resolve all one's problems, but to be in peace. In this I agree with Etty Hillesum, who said in 1942: "Ultimately, we have just one duty: to reclaim large areas of peace in ourselves, more and more peace, and to reflect it toward others. And the more peace there is in us, the more peace there will also be in our troubled world."[1]

If my heart is not at peace, I will be vulnerable to the full force of those divisions, those spirals of fear and violence that agitate the world. Everything that isn't peaceful

---

1. Etty Hillesum, *Etty*, pp. 535–536.

in me gives rise to evil; it is like an open door for demons, for forces of division that want to drag the world down to its ruin.

This was shown all too often in the course of the twentieth century: we saw many people, be they in Europe or Rwanda, even those calling themselves Christians—sometimes very involved in the Church—drawn to commit acts of violence or cowardice of which they would never have thought themselves capable. The underlying reason is that when the human heart is not really made peaceful by God, when it is still inhabited by fears and defense mechanisms, when we're still immersed in surroundings where evil is unleashed, where violence, hate, and partisan attitudes are spreading and social pressure grows ever stronger and stronger, we become incapable of resisting and let ourselves be led into committing evil. At certain historical junctures, good morals no longer suffice.

We must therefore keep ourselves ready, as Jesus says in the gospel, because we know neither the day nor the hour. For me, an essential aspect of this spiritual vigilance is to guard over our hearts and then learn to remain in God's peace, whatever happens.

Peacemakers come seventh among the Beatitudes in St. Matthew's gospel. The number seven indicates completion, fullness, crowning. The person envisaged by the Beatitude resounds with peace. In the Latin liturgy, the word "peace" is found seven times between the Our Father and Communion. The Eucharist is the heart's purification place par excellence, a repose in God.

If we take the path of the Beatitudes, each of them an expression of spiritual poverty (docility, affliction, hunger and thirst for justice, mercy, purity of heart), the fruit attained is peace of heart, which permits us to become peacemakers for those around us and truly to merit the title of children of God. Only the acquisition of this peace permits us to live the eighth Beatitude—to accept persecution joyfully and not as a disgrace.

Interior Peace, a Divine Promise

Acquiring peace, even if it takes a lot of work, is more about welcoming a promise than an ascetic exercise. Jesus' long discourse in the Gospel of John after the Last Supper is very significant in this regard. It begins like this, at the start of chapter 14: "Let not your hearts be troubled" (Jn 14:1). A little bit later, Jesus says: "Peace I leave with you; my peace I give to you; not as the world gives do I give to you. Let not your hearts be troubled, neither let them be afraid" (Jn 14:27).

The peace promised by Jesus is not that of the world (the tranquility when all goes well, when problems are resolved and desires satisfied, a peace that is, after all, rather rare). Rather, the peace Jesus promises can be received and experienced even in situations that are catastrophic by human standards—because its source and foundation is in God. At the end of chapter 16 of the Gospel, just before the priestly prayer to the Father, Jesus' last words to the disciples are these: "I have said this to you, that in me you may have peace. In the world you have tribulation; but be of good cheer, I have overcome the world" (Jn 16:33). It seems as if the ultimate goal of all of Jesus' words, his spiritual testament, was to establish peace in the believer.

Our peace doesn't come from the world, from exterior circumstances. It comes from our communion in faith and love with Jesus, the Prince of Peace. It is the fruit of prayer. God is an ocean of peace, and each time we are in intimate union with him through prayer, our hearts find peace again. Sometimes praying until peace comes back is an urgent duty. I think the experience of prayer as a place of peace is one of the criteria of authentic discernment in our prayer life. It doesn't matter if our prayer seems arid: if it brings us the fruits of peace, it will cease to have this effect and will become a place to pose questions.

One of the beautiful Scripture texts showing this peace promise (there are many) occurs in the Letter to the Philippians. "The Lord is at hand. Have no anxiety about anything, but in everything by prayer and supplication with thanksgiving let your requests be made known to God. And the peace of God, which passes all understanding, will keep your hearts and your minds in Christ Jesus" (Phil 4:5–7).

Why Look for Interior Peace?

The quest for interior peace is much more than the search for peace of mind. It really is about something else: opening ourselves up to God's actions. It's important to understand a simple but spiritually important truth: the more we reach out toward peace, the more the grace of God is capable of acting in our lives. Like a tranquil lake perfectly reflects the sun, so is a peaceful heart receptive to the action and movement of the Spirit. "The devil is ever solicitous to banish peace from your mind, knowing well that God only dwells there in peace, and that it is in peace that he works his wonders."[2] St. Francis de Sales said the

2. Lorenzo Scupoli, *Spiritual Combat* (Manchester: R. W. Dean & Co, 1801), p. 66. Scupoli was an author of the sixteenth century who greatly influenced St. Francis de Sales.

same thing to one of his followers in a letter of spiritual direction, urging her to keep a tranquil heart. Only a peaceful heart is capable of truly loving.

Remaining calm in the face of trouble, uneasiness, and interior disturbances is necessary in order for God to act in our lives. We can still grow in love, and our lives can have the fruitfulness we are called to have if we can accomplish this inward peace.

I would add that the only time we have good discernment is when we are at peace. When we're preoccupied by worry, disturbed by events in our lives, our emotions can get the best of us and we don't have an objective grasp on reality—we are tempted to see everything in black and white and question everything in our life. On the other hand, when we are at peace we see life clearly. St. Ignatius of Loyola understood this, distinguishing periods of "consolation" and "desolation" in the spiritual life, and he invites us not to make life-changing decisions in the latter case but exhorts us to remain faithful to what we determined during the last peaceful period.

We should adopt the following rule of conduct: when a problem has robbed us of our peace, the most important thing is not to resolve the problem in the hope of regaining our peace, but to regain a minimum of peacefulness, and then to see what we can do to face the problem. We will avoid making irrational choices for all the wrong reasons. How do we get back this minimum level of peace? Essentially through prayer, listening to the Word, and believing that God will never abandon us.

The Long Work of Reconciliation

Besides those "timely" actions required in the troubled moments just mentioned, acquiring interior peace also requires that we devote ourselves to a deeper effort that ultimately sums up the whole Christian life. It is to note everything not at peace within us and, being open to grace, discern a path of simultaneous healing and conversion, allowing us to be less and less the playthings of exterior circumstances or of our own wounds and find greater stability in God. Here we have a vast field of work for which this brief reflection can give only a few pointers.

It is interesting that the word "peace" in Hebrew tradition, whose first meaning signifies the opposite of war, also indicates achievement, fullness, abundance. Being at peace means being able to say with the psalmist, "The Lord is my shepherd, I shall not want" (Ps 23:1). Here, then, the opposite of peace is want, frustration, emptiness, dissatisfaction. The two meanings are linked: most of the time it's our wants and frustrations that nourish conflicts with others. We can't put up with them because we can't put up with ourselves.

Nothing is as opposed to peace in its biblical sense as an interior void, the dissatisfaction arising from a life without meaning. Mankind is called to happiness, destined for fullness, made to be whole; the sense of emptiness is intolerable. In today's world, it's easy to see how a spiritual void can be destructive: it engenders violence or depression, or even a frenetic quest to fill the void. Modern man is menaced more than ever by a whole series of addictive behaviors (sex, alcohol, drugs, Internet, food), which generally begin with an illusory attempt to fill a want.

Notice, too, that, if peace is opposed to conflict, then not all wars are overt wars involving manifest violence or aggression. Besides these offensive wars, there also are defensive wars waged with weapons like fearful conduct, turning in on one's self, efforts to control everything, and the raising of barriers to protect oneself, others, or life itself. This is also the opposite of biblical peace.

And so the acquisition of true interior peace must be accompanied by self-awareness and an openness to divine grace in relation to all the attitudes and conduct (more or less conscious) mentioned here. We must face up to our aggressions, our angers, our hatred, and our bitterness, but also to our frustrations, dissatisfactions, fears, denial or defense mechanisms, and refusals to live, for these are expressions of a lack of peace and nourish the conflicts in which we all too often find ourselves enmeshed.

Schematically, we can distinguish four domains in which a lack of peace manifests itself:

Relationship with God. To be at peace with God shows an attitude of availability, of confidence, of gratitude. Sometimes we can flee him, close ourselves up, mistrust him. We can blame him for some suffering we've lived through, such as a trial we've undergone, or a seemingly sterile faithfulness. We can feel unworthy or culpable before him.

Relationship with one's self. Not accepting ourselves as we are is a frequent experience: judging ourselves, detesting ourselves, being perpetually discontent with ourselves.

Relationship with others. Lack of peace in relationships is evidenced by fears and barriers and also bitterness, grudges, and forgiveness spurned.

And I would add: *lack of peace in our relationship with existence, with life.* It can take the form of regretting the past, worrying about the future, feeling overburdened in the present life, and losing our feeling or taste for what we are experiencing now.

All this is to say that the acquisition of interior peace presupposes a lengthy work of reconciliation: reconciliation with God, with ourselves and our weakness, with our neighbor, with life. Though a laborious task, which demands patience and perseverance, it is eminently possible, since it is exactly for this work of reconciliation that Christ was given to us in that he came to make peace through the blood of the Cross. Reconciling mankind with God while showing us the true image of the Father, he reconciles human beings little by little with themselves, with their neighbors, and with life itself. Only Christ is our peace, just as St. Paul affirms in the Letter to the Ephesians, because we have in Christ "access in one Spirit to the Father" (Eph 2:14–18).

CHAPTER 6

In Quest of Identity

Social Recognition in Crisis

Students of today's society notice a certain contradiction. On the one hand, people appear to have an ever-increasing need for recognition. Nearly everyone aspires to be recognized, to overcome anonymity, to be a subject of discussion: dreams of becoming celebrities have never been as strong as they are now. Consider the success of *People* magazine, participation in televised games and beauty contests, the drive for sports records of all sorts (published each year in *Guinness World Records*, where one finds such remarkable items as the record for ingesting scorpions), and the proliferation of blogs, to name just a few. One drawing by Sempé [a French cartoonist] shows a little man in an immense library, its shelves filled to the ceiling with thousands of volumes, looking up from writing and saying to a friend: "I've decided to write a novel to emerge from anonymity!"

On the other hand, institutions that used to be able to confer a certain character or recognition on individuals are hard put to do that today. In the family sphere, the parental image is discredited. Schools are derided; college diplomas no longer guarantee a job. In the political world, government and civic honors are suspect, at best. The job security of a company's CEO depends on the whim of stockholders and the bottom line more than the value of his work, and economic pressures often make professional life a source of anguish over gratification. Military life is of little interest, while Western secular culture regards the representatives of religion and morality as having nothing important to say. Vice is more fashionable than virtue, and few people look up to the clergy anymore.

And so we face this paradox: a cruel hunger for recognition and esteem at a time when there is no one in a position to confer them. All that remains is public opinion or media, whose recognition is ephemeral—based on superficial values and passing styles incapable of making anyone happy.

Fragile Emotional Recognition

The unsatiated need for social recognition is often transferred to the private sphere, the sphere of interpersonal relationships. Seeking emotional warmth, we create a refuge in our private lives: think how teenagers stick together. We also see an extreme emphasis on the experience of love. It's true that romantic love has a very beautiful aspect: one face among all others acquires a unique value in my eyes, and I become someone unique for another person. Mutual recognition and reciprocal appreciation (in the etymological sense: to give value) takes place. Each acquires immense value for the other, and discovering the other, I am revealed to myself. This experience of being loved in a unique way meets a profound need. But it is fragile and doesn't always keep its promises. If the need for recognition is nourished exclusively by emotional relationships, what happens to it when the feeling of love gives way to indifference, to rejection? Everything crumbles. Satisfying the need for recognition calls for a more solid foundation than interpersonal relationships alone. For how can a being similar to me, fragile and imperfect, confer on me true recognition on its own? This requires the mediation of an Other.

These paradoxes are resolved in an encounter with the Father. He alone can give the recognition for which each of us thirsts. Only he reveals to each person his true identity, simultaneously doing it with the greatest objective truth and subjective tenderness possible. Deepening one's filial relationship with God generates in the human heart the nucleus of personal identity, solid and gentle: a double certainty—of being loved and of being able to love. Both are necessary, and it's only through living by the gift of the Spirit as a child of God that people find their ultimate foundation.

Psychological Personality

The thirst for identity can be seen in the current infatuation with psychology. Consider today's penchant for tests. Women's magazines regularly publish quizzes that supposedly provide the answer to crucial questions like "What kind of lover are you?"

But psychological tests, no matter how sophisticated, in the end shed light on what is only a superficial aspect of personality. At best, they identify a person as fitting into some category. One has been put in a box or given a number, but nothing is said concerning what is really singular about a person. In the quest for and construction of identity, psychology has an undeniable usefulness: it permits us to "clear the ground," to help a person perceive vanishing hopes or what is artificial in his or her notion of "me" (illusions, dependencies in relation to the expectations of others, and so forth). But it doesn't give access to the person's profound identity.

The Father Who Makes Us His Children

More broadly, in the development of personal identity, the human dimensions are of course very important (discovery and use of talents and strengths, the praise they receive from others), but what is decisive in the end is the spiritual dimension, the establishment of a true and profound relationship with God grounded in accepting and putting into practice of the word: "Thou art my beloved Son; with thee I am well pleased" (Mk 1:11). God, in revealing his fatherly face, hands over to us human beings the task of discovering our own faces. The discovery of one's profound identity is really and truly a revelation. Revealing himself as Creator, Savior, Father, God reveals mankind to itself. To each of us he reveals what is unique about us: the unique love with which God loves each one and also the unique love one can give to God and to the world—a love that no other person can give in one's place. I will never be St. Francis or St. Teresa of Calcutta, but, as many saints wanted, I can love God as no one has ever yet loved him. I have a unique way of keeping God's image in me, configuring myself to Christ, and being fruitful.

But be aware of this. The process by which someone accesses his or her profound identity, a true self-knowledge of his or her mission and the grace that goes with it, is far from being a tranquil, linear process of progressively acquiring qualities, competences, and so on. It is often paradoxical, in the logic of the gospel: one must be lost to be found. There will be many trials, failures, humiliations, painful austerities, and even lamentable falls (as happened with St. Peter). It is a way that throws light on the poverty and radical helplessness that is our lot. This is necessary so that the artificial and willful part of our identity, composed of presumptions, illusions, narcissism, and egocentric quests that reside in us all, is radically eliminated. The superficial "me" must die so that one's true identity is revealed. Paradoxically, it is in accepting one's poverty that we discover the marvel that we are in the eyes of God. But we must go through deep levels of misery to discover the holy and intact kernel of our personality, which is no other than God's singular love for us and the singular love that, out of pure grace, he gives us the possibility of sharing.

Those who, at the heart of their poverty, look ceaselessly for God and respond sincerely to his calls, will sooner or later and by making their own the words of Psalm 139: "I praise thee, for thou art fearful and wonderful. . . . Thou knowest me right well" (Ps 139:14).

CHAPTER 7

Eucharist and Faith

The Year of the Eucharist

In declaring 2004 a Year of the Eucharist, St. John Paul II was extending an invitation to be taken very seriously. The Holy Father himself considered it to be a synthesis and summit of the Church's path in the preceding ten years since *Tertio Millennio Adveniente*, which he published in anticipation of the Jubilee Year 2000.

The Eucharist is not just a sacrament to be celebrated. It also must be the focus of our lives and the source of our internal renewal. In the apostolic letter *Mane Nobiscum Domine* (Stay with us, Lord), introducing the Year of the Eucharist, the Holy Father described the Eucharist as a "mode of being, which passes from Jesus into each Christian."[1] He called on Christians to

---

1. John Paul II, *Mane Nobiscum Domine*, Apostolic Letter to the Bishops, Clergy, and Faithful for the Year of the Eucharist, 7 October 2004, 25, *www.vatican.va*.

embrace that reality, be proud our faith, and, by their witness, promote a "culture of the Eucharist"[2] that would serve to nourish, strengthen, and renew the life of all Christians.

Much could be said about what the Eucharist, lived with faith and interiority, teaches and what attitudes it progressively fosters. It teaches us to make human life an act of thanksgiving and praise offered up to God: "The Eucharist has been given to us so that our life, like that of Mary, may become completely a *Magnificat!*"[3] It teaches us that mankind is called to nourish itself with God, that men are in communion with God and one another. It is an authentic school of charity, of life redeemed by love, of sharing, of service, of attention to the most poor. It is a *"great school of peace,"* as the Holy Father said.[4] Let's be clear that the Eucharist isn't only teaching and light to illuminate the path but is also grace, an interior transformation, and the strength to put all these attitudes into practice.

---

2. John Paul II, *Mane Nobiscum Domine*, 26.

3. John Paul II, *Ecclesia de Eucharistia*, Encyclical on the Eucharist in Its Relationship to the Church, 17 April 2013, 58, *www.vatican.va*.

4. John Paul II, *Mane Nobiscum Domine*, 27.

The Eucharist, School of Spiritual Maturity and of Faith

Christian maturity lies in making our own the attitudes of faith, hope, and love. The theological virtues, as they are traditionally called, are to become, little by little, the foundation of our very being, even to the point of progressively restructuring our psychological makeup. I want now to explain how the Eucharist is a very precious education for us in faith, hope, and love. First I shall speak of faith, later of the other two.

Mysterium Fidei

One of the primary characteristics of the Eucharist is that it is a mystery of faith. Only faith can truly immerse us in the understanding of this great sacrament. This doesn't mean naive credulity, with reason silenced. Faith and reason absolutely need each other and mutually support each other, as St. John Paul II reminded us in his encyclical *Fides et Ratio*. Reason without faith is at risk of becoming enclosed in a narrow vision of the world, while faith without reason can't satisfy our need to bring intelligence into play in seeking to understand what we believe as much as possible and to support the growth of faith.

Still, it is true that only faith gives us access to the deepest truths about the Eucharist. This mystery, St. John Paul II said, "taxes our mind's ability to pass beyond appearances. Here our senses fail us: *visus, tactus, gustus in te fallitur*, in the words of the hymn *Adoro Te Devote*; yet faith alone, rooted in the word of Christ handed down to us by the Apostles, is sufficient for us."[5]

When St. John Paul II spoke of Mary in *Ecclesia de Eucharistia*, the first trait that he evoked was Mary's faith: "If the Eucharist is a mystery of faith which so greatly transcends our understanding as to call for sheer abandonment to the word of God, then there can be no one like Mary to act as our support and guide in acquiring this disposition."[6]

Frequenting the Eucharist fosters an attitude of faith in us. It teaches us not to trust in mere appearances but to make the Word of God the grounding of our perception of reality, with confidence in the truth of this Word. It obliges us not to remain at the level of our impressions but to take seriously this Word and the divine universe to which it gives access.

---

5. John Paul II, *Ecclesia de Eucharistia*, 59.

6. John Paul II, *Ecclesia de Eucharistia*, 54.

That helps us to get beyond rationalism, which imagines that the only reality is what reason can grasp by its own resources and traps us in a narrow, suffocating view of the world. This rationalist tendency has had a strong grip on the Western world for the past several centuries, but lately it has provoked a reaction, visible in the fascination with the paranormal, horoscopes, magic, and so on. Why were the Harry Potter books so popular? Because people need mystery and cannot be contented with a universe reduced to what logic and reason are able to comprehend. The paradox of contemporary culture is its constant oscillation between narrow rationalism and fascination for the most obscure and most dangerous realm of the irrational. We would do better to remain within the Christian tradition, where the need for the marvelous, the mysterious, and the transcendental coexists comfortably with realism and the demands of reason.

Entering into the Wisdom of God

Supported by confidence in God's Word and promises, accustomed by the Eucharist to seeing reality with the eyes of faith, we avoid allowing ourselves to be confined within a solely human wisdom and security. We are constantly tempted to judge all reality by appearances or our own criteria, thus remaining incapable of entering into God's wisdom and discerning his action. The result is that we are worried and forever discouraged, since instead of taking God's promises seriously, we prefer to trust in ourselves and our limited perceptions of the world.

Our most urgent need is to increase our faith. Sometimes I say jokingly that the only real problem in the end is lack of faith. All other problems, confronted with faith, are not so much problems as occasions of human spiritual growth. "Everything is a grace," said St. Thérèse, not long before her death.[7] Even the worst difficulties, lived in faith and hope, sooner or later turn to our advantage, disclosing hidden treasures more beautiful and precious than any we could have devised on our own.

The day we understand this will mark a great victory. We will be at peace with life. We will be more accepting of ourselves and our personal histories—more accepting, too, of others and more at peace with them. No longer will we find it necessary to spend our lives looking for others to blame or inventing scapegoats responsible for our unhappiness.

---

7. Thérèse of Lisieux, *Her Last Conversations*, June 5.4.

Faith Discovers the Most Real of Realities

Venerating the Eucharist is a way for us to strongly confess our faith in the truth of the Word of God and to make that faith grow. Here we discover that faith gives us access to reality. What we believe—even if it is sometimes partially obscured by our reason and puzzling to our senses—herein reveals itself as the supreme reality, a reality that doesn't disappoint us but instead fulfills us beyond all expectations. Baldwin of Ford, a Cistercian of the twelfth century marveled that from the beginning of time, Christ was hidden: first in the bosom of the Father, then in the form of a slave, and now in the sacrament that he instituted. "Faith finds him hidden in the bosom of the Father; no less does faith find him hidden in man; and it is faith which finds him hidden" in the sacrament of the altar.[8]

The celebration of the Eucharist, lived with faith and with love, and the hours spent in silent meditation before the Blessed Sacrament all are certain finally to bring us to a true experience of God in which we see clearly that we are approaching the ultimate reality. Sometimes, paradoxically, this mystery so poor and confusing in appearances

---

8. Sommerfeldt, John R., *Erudition at God's Service* (Kalamazoo, Mich.: Cistercian Publications, 1987), p. 221.

gives us moments of fullness and happiness surpassing anything earth can bestow. In *Mane Nobiscum Domine*, St. John Paul II spoke of an experience of the saints (and no doubt also his own): "How many times did they shed tears of profound emotion in the presence of this great mystery, or experience hours of inexpressible 'spousal' joy before the sacrament of the altar!"[9] The Eucharist permits us sooner or later to "taste and see that the Lord is good!" as Psalm 34 says; it places us in contact with the most real of realities: the God-Love.

I am persuaded that this sanctifying experience is destined to be the experience of all believers. In years to come, there will be more Eucharistic miracles, not necessarily extraordinary manifestations but hearts transformed and psyches healed by contact with the Eucharist.

Through love of the Eucharist we discover that an act of faith opens us to unexpected realities, which, although mysterious and puzzling to our human faculties, are no less solidly real, true reference points for our interior transformation and our human and spiritual growth. St. Paul congratulated the Colossians for the "firmness of your faith" (Col 2:5). Faith will always remain in some sense a leap into the unknown. But faith is firm, because

---

9. John Paul II, *Mane Nobiscum Domine*, 31.

the realities to which it gives access cannot deceive us. On the contrary, they fulfill us, make us live, and renew us internally from day to day. The "righteous one shall live by faith" (Heb 10:38). And the Church to come will find wisdom and extraordinary vitality in its Eucharistic faith.

CHAPTER 8

Eucharist and Hope

Eucharist, Happiness of the Poor and Hope for the Kingdom to Come

In showing how the celebration of the Eucharist is a school of spiritual maturity, increasing the theological virtues of faith, hope, and charity, I began by showing how it fosters an attitude of faith in us and helps us experience how faith gives us access to wonderful, fruitful realities. Now I turn to the link between the Eucharist and hope.

Hope is the confident expectation of the realization of God's promises. It turns us joyfully toward the world to come, the glory to which we are heirs in Christ, a glory without measure compared to the present sufferings. Hope also is the virtue that leads us to accept poverty, never worried or discouraged by our weakness, but accepting everything in the mercy and love of God. Let's examine these two aspects of hope.

Hope and Spiritual Poverty

Hope is an attribute of the heart that helps us confidently await God's gifts while accepting our spiritual poverty. It is expressed and lived in a special way in the celebration and adoration of the Eucharist.

To understand this, we must understand the strong link between poverty and hope. We really can't "go forward in hope," according to St. John Paul II's invitation,[1] unless we are poor of spirit. To the extent we have riches or place our trust in security and human support, we can't really practice hope, which consists in counting on God alone. God sometimes permits us to go through trials, the loss of some of our security, even lamentable falls, in order that we learn in the end to count on nothing but him and his mercy. Peter is a good example: he had to fall, denying Christ during his Passion, in order to learn not to lean on his own virtues, his own courage, the momentum of human enthusiasm, but only on the love of Jesus.

Even in the spiritual domain, we are always tempted by riches: we want to be sure of ourselves, to have abundant "stocks" of grace, virtues, formation, and wisdom to

---

1. John Paul II, *Novo Millennio Inuente*, Apostolic Letter to the Bishops, the Clergy, and the Faithful at the Close of the Great Jubilee Year 2000, 6 January 2001, 58. *www.vatican.va*.

support us so we can calmly confront life's difficulties. By definition, however, grace is not kept in reserve. It is humbly received day by day. It's like the manna that fed the Hebrews in the desert: when you try to preserve it, it spoils. We must gather it up each day. This is not to say there's no need to exercise virtue and grow, but we must not lean on ourselves and create false security in doing so. In the Our Father, when we confide our needs to God (who knows them better than we do!), we do not ask for a store of bread; we ask for the bread for each day—just what's necessary for today, forgetting the past and not worrying about tomorrow. "Therefore do not be anxious about tomorrow, for tomorrow will be anxious for itself. Let the day's own trouble be sufficient for the day," the gospel tells us (cf. Mt 6:34).

Embracing hope, then, implies acceptance of our weakness and poverty, living in a sort of permanent precariousness, without genuinely satisfying human support, neither within us nor without, yet at the same time possessing a limitless confidence in the faithfulness and bounty of God.

This attitude, in the end, is a source of much freedom and joy. Freedom, since the more we rely on our own riches, the more we work with a certain amount of worry, fearful of losing one thing or another, and tempted to indulge in ceaseless calculation and measurement, while we're never really free. Joy, since someone who looks to God for everything knows the happiness of experiencing his faithfulness and day by day receiving everything necessary from the hand of one who loves us and whom we love. Thus the heart is filled with gratitude and love.

Eucharist, Richness of the Poor

The Eucharist is, as it were, the manna that feeds us in our destitution in the desert, giving us just what is necessary—neither more nor less—day by day.

The Church's liturgy has always liked to use Psalm 23 as a Communion hymn. Many of its verses can be interpreted in reference to the Eucharistic mystery. It speaks of a meal: "Thou preparest a table before me in the presence of my enemies; thou anointest my head with oil, my cup overflows" (Ps 23:5). There is the joy of the Divine Presence: "Surely goodness and mercy shall follow me all the days of my life; and I shall dwell in the house of the Lord for ever" (Ps 23:6). Its opening words: "The Lord is my Shepherd, I shall not want," form one of the most beautiful prayers we can say after receiving Communion. Thanks to this Communion, I lack nothing. I am certain God has given me absolutely everything necessary for today. Said Fr. Jean-Claude Sagne: "The Eucharist is the gift of God in his fullness, it gives to us everything that we need to accomplish God's will in giving us ourselves."[2] If we have this faith, God will respond to our confidence, and Communions will be even more fruitful. "According to your faith, let it be done to you," Jesus often says in the Gospel (Mt 9:29; see also Mt 8:13, Lk 8:48).

In the Second Letter to the Corinthians, Paul tells us: "God is able to provide you with every blessing in abundance, so that you may always have enough of everything and may provide in abundance for every good work" (2 Cor 9:8). Nowhere is that more true than in the Eucharist, where the resplendent mystery of the love of God, who made himself incredibly poor for us, enriches us with the fullness of his love and his life. What an awesome exchange—the poorness of God becomes our richness!

In Eucharistic adoration, the act of gathering like poor ones before Jesus, who is so poor—there's little else we can do there—helps us to accept our poverty and transforms it into a place for welcoming the gift of God, who is, in the end, our only wealth. Fr. Sagne said of adoration:

---

2. Jean-Claude Sagne, *L'itinéraire spirituel du couple: Le Mystère de l'amour dans le mariage* (Saint-Paul: Chemin Neuf, 2001).

Source and end of all Christian prayer, adoration is the engagement of the person himself, at the special place where we reach the limit of acts and words. Adoration unfolds on a foundation of accepted poverty. . . . Adoration is the prayer of the poor: "Open your mouth wide, and I will fill it." (Ps 81:10)[3]

Eucharist and the Hope for the Kingdom

When Peter speaks to the leaders of the churches—of whom he is one—he reminds them that a minister of the Church, before assuming a ministry, is first of all someone who has had a spiritual experience: "So I exhort the elders among you, as a fellow elder and a witness of the sufferings of Christ as well as a partaker in the glory that is to be revealed" (1 Pt 5:1). He knew fervent love of God manifested in the sufferings of Christ, and that led him to live in the fullness of hope for the glory and beauty of the world to come.

We encounter these two realities in the Eucharist. It is the reminder that makes the Lord's Passion present today (during each Mass, we are mystically the contemporaries of the Cross), but it is also the anticipated presence of the

---

3. Jean-Claude Sagne, *L'itinéraire spirituel du couple*.

world to come. The Eucharist makes us participants in the sufferings of Christ while making us part of the glory and happiness of the next life. It orients and nourishes the hope of the Christian. It intensifies our desire for the Second Coming. "We await the blessed hope and the coming of our Savior, Jesus Christ," as the Eucharistic liturgy says after the Our Father. The Eucharist, celebrated with fervor, makes this hope more and more a certainty that strengthens our commitments here below. Nothing is more enlivening than hope! Despair or worry quickly diminishes the generosity of love.

In his apostolic letter *Mane Nobiscum Domine*, St. John Paul II wrote:

> While the Eucharist makes present what occurred in the past, it also *impels us towards the future, when Christ will come again* at the end of history. This "eschatological" aspect makes the Sacrament of the Eucharist an event which draws us into itself and fills our Christian journey with hope.[4]

The Holy Father also expressed beautifully the link between the Eucharistic celebration and the future kingdom:

4. John Paul II, *Mane Nobiscum Domine*, 15.

This relationship of profound and mutual "abiding" *enables us to have a certain foretaste of heaven on earth.* Is this not the greatest of human yearnings? Is this not what God had in mind when he brought about in history his plan of salvation? God has placed in human hearts a "hunger" for his word (cf. *Am* 8:11), a hunger which will be satisfied only by full union with him. Eucharistic communion was given so that we might be "sated" with God here on earth, in expectation of our complete fulfillment in heaven.[5]

Hope plays a key role in the dynamism of the spiritual life. Founded on faith, it permits the blossoming of charity. It purifies the heart, according to the beautiful expression of St. John: "Every one who thus hopes in him purifies himself as he is pure" (1 Jn 3:3). And so it permits us to see God at work. As St. John of the Cross said (in words that delighted the little Thérèse), it is the source of all the graces: "the soul obtains from God as much as it hopes for him."[6] God doesn't give according to our merit, our virtues, or our qualities, but according to our hope in him, our confidence in his mercy. There is an immense consolation and freedom in understanding that.

---

5. John Paul II, *Mane Nobiscum Domine*, 19.

6. John of the Cross, *Dark Night of the Soul* (Mineola, N.Y.: Dover, 2003), p. 101. Kindle edition.

May each of our Eucharistic celebrations be, then, an occasion to manifest and nourish the joyful "pride in our hope" (Heb 3:6) that must dwell in the heart of every Christian. To maintain a joyful outlook on all things is perhaps the greatest service believers can provide for today's world.

CHAPTER 9

Eucharist and Love

The fundamental dynamism of Christian life, as we know, consists in the practice of faith, hope, and charity, with the Eucharist as source and summit of the Church's life, expressing and nourishing these three theological virtues. Up to now, I have spoken of the link between Eucharist, faith, and hope. Here I want to consider the link between Eucharist and charity. That the Eucharist is the sacrament of charity above all—expressing and nourishing of the love of God as well as love of neighbor—is an incontrovertible truth. Nonetheless, this truth merits closer attention.

Sacrament of God's Love

The Eucharist is the highest expression of divine charity, of God's love for his creations. Through it, God shows how much he wants to be with us forever, sharing his own life with us, living with us and in us. As Fr. Jean-Claude Sagne said, "What makes the Eucharist the sacrament of love is that Jesus here gives himself in person, in the fullness of his presence. He gives all that he is, the entirety of his life. More than any word or action, it is Jesus himself who comes to us and delivers himself into our hands. The Eucharist is a giving without limits on Jesus' part: 'This is my body, given up for you.'"[1] What we receive in the Eucharist is Jesus in the very act of giving his life for all mankind, the act in which he personally loves each of us with the greatest of loves: "Greater love has no man than this, that a man lay down his life for his friends" (Jn 15:13). Each time we receive the Eucharist, we should be moved with the same awe that St. Paul had, in knowing: "[he] loved me and gave himself for me" (Gal 2:20).

In *Ecclesia de Eucharistia*, St. John Paul II reminds us that in the Eucharist "we can say not only that *each one of us receives Christ*, but also that *Christ receives each one of us*."[2] There we have all the dynamism of love as a welcoming and a gift at the same time, for to love someone is to welcome him or her into your life. These two movements are deeply linked: Isn't the biggest gift

---

1. Jean-Claude Sagne, *L'itinéraire spirituel du couple*.

2. John Paul II, *Ecclesia de Eucharistia*, 22.

we can give someone to accept him or her as he or she is? Fr. Sagne correctly notes: "If the biggest desire of love is to remain with the other, to find an abode in the other's heart—and for that to make of oneself an abode for the loved one—the Eucharist is the sacrament of love par excellence. Jesus once again makes his heart a welcoming abode for all mankind."[3] This is the profound truth announced in the Gospel of John: "He who eats my flesh and drinks my blood abides in me, and I in him" (Jn 6:56). St. Catherine of Siena used an amusing image to express this. By receiving Communion, she said, the soul dwells in God and God in the soul, "as the fish is in the sea and the sea in the fish," so [is God] in the soul and the soul in [God], the sea of peace.[4]

The Eucharist makes clear the degree of intimacy into which God wants to draw us. In the Eucharist, the mad dream of all lovers is realized: to be one in being with the object of our love. God lets himself be eaten by us; he becomes our substance, and at the same time, he draws us out of ourselves to make us his. Here is an interesting reflection by Pope Benedict XVI in a homily to a Eucharistic congress in Bari, Italy: "Christ is truly present

---

3. Jean-Claude Sagne, *L'itinéraire spirituel du couple.*

4. Catherine of Siena, *The Dialogue*, trans. Suzanne Noffke, OP (New York: Paulist Press, 1980), p. 112.

among us in the Eucharist. His presence is not static. It is a dynamic presence that grasps us, to make us his own, to make us assimilate him. Christ draws us to him, he makes us come out of ourselves to make us all one with him."[5]

St. Augustine understood this well. Educated in Neoplatonism, he found it difficult to accept the incarnational dimension of Christianity. In particular, he reacted against the idea of a "Eucharistic meal," which seemed to him to be unworthy of God. In normal everyday meals, we are the strong ones, since we assimilate the food and make it part of our own bodily reality. Only later did St. Augustine understand that in the Eucharist, it is the other way around: Christ draws us to himself, making us one single thing with him.

The Eucharist means nourishing ourselves with God, but also—if we may say so—letting ourselves be devoured by him!

God Gives Us to Give of Ourselves

The real excellence of the Eucharist lies in the fact that God not only gives us his love but gives us the gift of loving in return. Through it, he empowers us to respond to

---

5. Benedict XVI, *Homily for the Closing of the 24th Italian National Eucharistic Congress*, 29 May 2005, *www.vatican.va*.

his love little by little, to love just as we have been loved by him. Here is a reminder of an essential property of love, ever expanding toward full reciprocity: to love someone is to give him or her the possibility of loving us back. The greatest gift we can give someone is the power of self-giving, to experience the happiness of giving ourselves through love, since "it is more blessed to give than to receive" (Acts 20:35; cf. Lk 6:34).

The Eucharist comes to the aid of our weakness. It transforms our hearts of stone into hearts of flesh, hearts capable of love—even God's love; it assimilates us and makes us conform to Christ little by little. It is like a security deposit, carrying with it the hope that one day we will be able to love God as he loves us, with the same truth, the same purity, the same strength, the same generosity. "Hope does not disappoint us, because God's love has been poured into our hearts through the Holy Spirit who has been given to us," St. Paul says in the Letter to the Romans (Rom 5:5).

Each Communion is a diffusion of the spirit of love into the hearts of the faithful. Through it we are in touch with Jesus' love for his Father, and we participate in Jesus' compassion and infinite tenderness toward every child of God. Here, Jesus comes secretly but truly, to live and love in us, communicating his interior disposition of docility and humility.

We should desire it intensely, while also waiting patiently for what the Eucharist sows within us to bear visible fruit, and knowing that it can produce very profound changes in our hearts. "He who eats my flesh and drinks my blood has eternal life" (Jn 6:54–56). And eternal life is no less than loving with God's own love.

Sacrament of Brotherly Love

Uniting us to Christ, the Eucharist also integrates us into the community of brotherly love. As the sacrament of God's love, the Eucharist is of course also a sacrament of love of others, of communion with our brothers and sisters. It expresses and effects people's most profound togetherness, making possible the kind of community that Christ makes possible in making us members of one body. "The cup of blessing which we bless, is it not a participation in the blood of Christ? The bread which we break, is it not a participation in the body of Christ? Because there is one bread, we who are many are one body, for we all partake of the one bread" (1 Cor 10:16).

St. John Chrysostom said this:

If it's the same body that nourishes us, and we all become this same body, why do we not also show the same love? Christ is united with you who are so far away, and you don't deign to unite yourself to your brother? . . . In fact, it isn't the case that one body is nourished by one member and another by another; it's the same body that nourishes all. That's why the apostle Paul added: 'we all share the same bread.' So then, if we all share the same bread, if we all become the same in Christ, why don't we show the same charity? . . . That's what we saw in the time of our fathers: 'the company of those who believed were of one heart and soul' (Acts 4:32). It isn't the same at the present; it's just the opposite. And yet, it's Christ who came to look for you, you who were so far from him, to unite himself to you. And you, you don't want to be united with your brother? . . . In fact, he didn't only give his body; but since the first flesh, drawn from the earth, was killed by sin, he introduced, in a sense, another leavening, his own flesh, of the same nature as ours but free from all sin, full of life. The Lord shared him with us all so that, nourished by this new flesh, each one in communion with the others, we can enter into eternal life.[6]

---

6. John Chrysostom, *Homilies on the First Letter to the Corinthians*, 24.

Writing to priests on Holy Thursday 2005, St. John
Paul II said:

> Christ's self-giving, which has its origin in the Trin-
> itarian life of the God who is Love, reaches its cul-
> mination in the sacrifice of the Cross, sacramentally
> anticipated in the Last Supper. It is impossible to
> repeat the words of consecration without *feeling one-
> self caught up in this spiritual movement.* In a certain
> sense, when he says the words "take and eat," the priest
> must learn to apply them also to himself, and to speak
> them with truth and generosity. If he is able to offer
> himself as a gift, placing himself at the disposal of the
> community and at the service of anyone in need, his
> life takes on its true meaning.[7]

What is true for priests is true for all the faithful.
In the Eucharist we nourish ourselves with Christ, to be
ourselves made ever more capable of being food for our
brothers and sisters, a response to their hunger for love.

The life of the little Thérèse of Lisieux is a powerful
example of how the Eucharist can transform one internally
and make him or her capable of the most heroic love. At
the age of fourteen, Thérèse had big expectations for a life

---

7. John Paul II, *Letter to Priests for Holy Thursday 2005*, 3, *www.vatican.va.*

filled with love, but she was humanly incapable of that—too entangled in her hypersensitivity, her timidity, her emotional fragility. Then God mercifully intervened in her life by the grace of Christmas. Thérèse described an experience that happened just after Midnight Mass, considering it a Christmas grace that was explicitly Eucharistic in nature. This Christmas grace made it possible for her to undertake an extraordinary growth in love, which Thérèse describes as follows: "The work I had been unable to do in ten years was done by Jesus in one instant, contenting himself with my *good will*. . . . He made me a fisher of *souls*. . . . I felt *charity* enter into my soul, and the need to forget myself and to please others; since then I've been happy!"[8]

The Sinners' Table

At the end of her life, Thérèse would undergo a terrible trial of faith, obsessed with horrible thoughts of doubt and disbelief. She offered up this trial for the atheists, who at the end of the nineteenth century were aggressively anticlerical and scornful. There is something Eucharistic in the way she expresses her acceptance of this trial for as long as God willed it:

---

8. Thérèse of Lisieux, *Story of a Soul*, p. 98.

Your child, O Lord, has understood Your divine light, and she begs pardon for her brothers. She is resigned to eat the bread of sorrow as long as you desire it; she does not wish to rise up from this table filled with bitterness at which poor sinners are eating until the day set by You. Can she not say in her name and in the name of her brothers, "Have pity on us, O Lord, for we are poor sinners! . . . Oh! Lord, send us away justified."[9]

How moving it is that the *us* with whom Thérèse identifies includes the worst enemies of the Church in her day. Like Jesus, she takes upon herself the sins of the world. There is no judging others, only immense compassion and complete solidarity with the sin of nonbelievers. Here is one aspect of the Eucharist's great mystery of mercy: Jesus at the sinners' table, offering his life and his body, making himself food that heals the sins of the world, by love offered the bread of misery (the expression used in the Jewish Passover meal) becomes the Bread of Life: "Behold, the Lamb of God, who takes away the sins of the world" (Jn 1:29)!

The Eucharist is at the same time a gift and an imperative, a call and a promise, responsibility and grace.

---

9. Thérèse of Lisieux, *Story of a Soul*, p. 212.

It is a powerful invitation to love as Jesus loves, to give one's life for our neighbor as he did. But it is also the assurance that one day, however great our weakness or misery may be, we will be raised to this height. The host we receive at Mass or adore in silence is humble as a mustard seed—and like a seed, it can blossom in our hearts into a tree where birds can come to nest and find solace. Like a little bit of leaven, it is capable of profoundly transforming our hearts, making loaves of bread that can satisfy much hunger.

CHAPTER 10

Come, Lord Jesus!

In the First Letter of St. Peter, we find this exhortation addressed to the elders of the Church (in Greek, the *presbyters*, which gives rise to the word *priest*): "So I exhort the elders among you, as a fellow elder and a witness of the sufferings of Christ as well as a partaker in the glory that is to be revealed. Tend the flock of God that is your charge, not by constraint but willingly, not for shameful gain but eagerly, not as domineering over those in your charge but being examples to the flock" (1 Pt 5:1–3).

One idea in this beautiful exhortation of St. Peter seems especially interesting to me. When the head of the apostles refers to himself in his own quality as an elder, he doesn't first define it in terms of function or task in the community. First he evokes a spiritual experience: he, an elder, is "witness of the sufferings of Christ" and is to participate in the glory that will be revealed. The role of elder appears first of all to have a double spiritual link:

to the Passion of the Lord and to the future glory of the Kingdom. Within this double spiritual link, those with responsibility in the Church find the strength needed to be good shepherds in Jesus' image, full of care, humility, and disinterested love toward those entrusted to them. Here is where one acquires pastoral charity. Even if this message concerns priests in particular, it has relevance for all Christians alike.

The elder is the "witness of the sufferings of Christ." Even if not a visual witness, as Peter, the elder, had been, someone who has attained true spiritual maturity deeply understands the mystery of the Lord's Passion. He or she has grasped the idea that what drove Jesus to accept the sufferings and outrages of the Cross was love beyond speaking. He or she has understood what an unending richness of mercy, of grace, of healing of hearts is contained in the wounds of the Lord. In the same letter, Peter evokes these "wounds [by which] you have been healed" (1 Pt 2:24). The elder is someone who remembers Jesus Christ, who constantly reminds us of Christ's suffering and Passion, and who brings together in this "memory" the desire to imitate Christ in giving of his or her life for friends and the necessary courage, despite weakness and poverty, to let himself or herself, little by little, be clothed in the very righteousness of Christ Jesus, as Paul indicates (see 2 Cor 5:21).

The elder is also someone who lives in the perspective of the future glory, who "reminds" us not only of the past but also of the future, which is certain, thus providing a foretaste of the happiness and glory that will be revealed when Christ returns. Peter did so in his second letter, evoking the day of the Transfiguration, when he was with the Lord on the holy mountain as an eyewitness of divine majesty, an experience that filled him with confidence in the power of Our Lord Jesus Christ and in his coming again (2 Pt 1:16–18). Filled with hope for the Kingdom, the elder inhabits, as it were, a new world crying out to be realized in splendor and beauty, and from this, he receives a powerful interior force. Having perceived with the eyes of the heart this "inheritance which is imperishable, undefiled, and unfading, kept in heaven for you," he trembles with joy (1 Pt 1:3–6).

Thus the activity of every minister of Christ is rooted in a double contemplation, a double communion, we might say, with the Passion of the Lord and with the glory of the world to come.

This double contemplation occurs and is deepened in a very special way in the liturgy of the Church. Meditation on the Word of God revives in us Christ's memory, which was announced by the prophets and the psalms and revealed in the Gospels. It also moves us to see the splendor of the heavenly Jerusalem, "prepared as a bride adorned for her husband" (Rv 21:2). This sort of contemplation is at its maximum intensity in the celebration of the Eucharist, memorial of the Passion of the Lord and guarantee of the glory to come.

At Mass, it is as if time is suspended: in faith we are made contemporaries of Christ's Cross, in a way hidden yet absolutely real. Just like those who were present at the event, we can take part in the sufferings of Christ and can be beneficiaries of the rivers of forgiveness and peace that spring from the Cross. Like the good thief, we can be purified by the blood of the Lamb without blemish, we can find our nourishment and our life in the mercy and love of God.

At each Eucharistic celebration, we are invited to take part in this Kingdom to come. In the bread and wine consecrated on the altar, the Kingdom of God is mysteriously but truly present in all its fullness and its richness, and we have access to it through faith. An anticipation of heavenly glory, the Eucharist makes present here below this kingdom of peace, of harmonious love, of sweetness and beauty which is the object of our peace—that new world to which we all aspire. Receiving it as a foretaste, we desire it all the more and say: "Maranatha! Come Lord

Jesus—let grace come, and let this world pass away!" as the old prayer of the Didache says.[1]

Each Eucharist, if lived with lively faith and fervent prayer, makes us taste how the Lord is good, how sweet it is to praise him and to love him, to live in his presence and share all together the same life and same love. It makes us yearn to manifest to all the world the glorious reality hidden in the humility of the sacramental species, veiled by appearances from our bodily eyes.

The Eucharist truly transports us to the heavens. Not in order to flee the realities of this world, but to give us a firm hope, to nourish our charity, and so give us the courage needed to assume the responsibilities of this life and enter into its struggles.

Here is the real condition for being an elder, here is real spiritual maturity: a deep faith that makes us share intimately in the Passion of the Lord and the glory of the world to come. It's this sharing that gives our present life all its fruitfulness. This was strongly experienced by the first Christian generation. They were still very close to the events of the Lord's life and waited for his imminent coming in glory, which they knew could be hastened through

---

1. See *The Fathers of the Church*, trans. Francis X. Glimm, Joseph M.-F. Marique, SJ, and Gerald G. Walsh, SJ (Washington, D.C.: The Catholic University of America Press, 2008), p. 180.

their prayers and desire. So the celebrations were marked with extraordinary fervor, which gave the Church great apostolic zeal.

After two thousand years and a certain dimming of the eschatological sense, all this may be more difficult for us. Yet the Spirit today invites us to regain this same spiritual intensity, this same mystic identification with the Cross and with glory, especially in our liturgies. May our celebrations move us to share with intense faith in the mystery of Christ handed down to us and in the splendor of the Kingdom to come, so that hope and charity may be renewed in us.

CHAPTER 11

Knowing God
through Mary

There is a magnificent promise in the Book of Isaiah: "The wolf shall dwell with the lamb, and the leopard shall lie down with the kid. . . . They shall not hurt or destroy in all my holy mountain; for the earth shall be full of the knowledge of the Lord as the waters cover the sea" (Is 11:6–9). This is a promise of knowledge of God that will accomplish a transformation of human hearts, a healing from evil and violence.

With all our being we should desire this knowledge of God, a knowledge he wants to reveal to us—not a God who is the product of our psychological projections, but the true living God. The Book of Job says: "I had heard of thee by the hearing of the ear, but now my eye sees thee" (Jb 42:5). We can all see God, discover his true face, not necessarily by visions and ecstasies but in a more humble and sure way: knowledge in faith.

Scripture says no one can see God. We will see him face-to-face only in another life. Yet here below we can have a true experience of God and know him. In the chapter 31 of the book of Jeremiah, we find another magnificent text on this subject:

> But this is the covenant which I will make with the house of Israel after those days, says the Lord: I will put my law within them, and I will write it upon their hearts; and I will be their God, and they shall be my people. And no longer shall each man teach his neighbor and each his brother, saying, "Know the Lord," for they shall all know me, from the least of them to the greatest, says the Lord; for I will forgive their iniquity, and I will remember their sin no more." (Jer 31:33–34)

This passage announces a knowledge of God by all, which will be intimately linked to the revelation of his mercy. The most profound knowledge of God we can have in this life comes through the experience of divine mercy, divine pardon. This Scripture promise is especially for us, in our times. God himself gives us that assurance: "All will know me, from the least of them to the greatest." I would even say especially the least! The Gospel of Luke tells of Jesus rejoicing in the joy of the Holy Spirit:

"I thank thee, Father, Lord of heaven and earth, that thou hast hidden these things from the wise and understanding and revealed them to babes; yea, Father, for such was thy gracious will. All things have been delivered to me by my Father; and no one knows who the Son is except the Father, or who the Father is except the Son and any one to whom the Son chooses to reveal him" (Lk 10:21–22).

It is through the Son that the revelation of the Father takes place. God wants to show his face to mankind. We have misrepresented God so much; heaped so much blame on him! This is the drama of atheism: throwing God into the trash, accusing him of being an enemy of mankind, an obstacle to freedom and flourishing, a God who crushes.

Today, more than ever, God wants to reveal himself to our hearts in a simple way, gently, in the mystery of faith, but still in a very profound way, such that each one of us can have an authentic knowledge of his true face. God wants to reveal himself more than ever to us small, poor beings.

One of the secret but favored paths of this revelation is the mystery of the Virgin Mary. It's beautiful to see how Mary is present today in the life of the world, gathering the hearts of men toward God, especially by schooling us in prayer. If we confide in her, if we let ourselves be led by her, she will lead us to a true knowledge of God by drawing us into the depths of prayer. Here is where God reveals himself, showing his face as Father. I recently spoke with some people about the experience of certain visionaries to whom Mary regularly appears in order to form them in person. The response of some was: "they're lucky." And no doubt they are. Yet I think Mary does this, secretly, for all who ask it of her. If we put everything totally in her hands, she will form us and will convey true knowledge of God to us. A poem on the Virgin by the little Thérèse called *Why I love you, O Mary*, contains this beautiful affirmation: "The treasures of a mother belong to her child."[1] To us Mary gives a share in that which is most precious: her faith.

In a beautiful passage in *The Secret of Mary*, Louis-Marie Grignion de Montfort said God is present everywhere and can be found everywhere, but in Mary he makes himself present to the small and the poor in a special way:

> Nowhere do we creatures find [God] nearer to us and more adapted to our weakness than in Mary, since it

---

1. Thérèse of Lisieux, *The Poetry of Saint Thérèse of Lisieux*, p. 153.

was for that end that He came and dwelt in her. Everywhere else he is the Bread of the strong, the Bread of the Angels, but in Mary He is the Bread of children.[2]

In Mary, God makes himself nourishment for the littlest ones. In her, we find God in his grandeur and majesty—his power, his wisdom that completely surpasses ours—yet at the same time an accessible God, not crushing us, not destroying us, but giving himself to be our life.

On May 13, 2000, during the beatification of the child visionaries of Fatima, Francisco and Jacinta, Pope St. John Paul II gave a beautiful homily in which he commented on the passage of Luke's gospel quoted earlier, saying that what God hid from the sages and the wise men he revealed to the littlest ones, like these children. The Holy Father evoked an experience of theirs during one of the apparitions of the Virgin:

According to the divine plan, "a woman clothed with the sun" (Rv 12:1) came down from heaven to this earth, to visit the privileged children of the Father. She speaks to them with a mother's voice and heart: she asks them to offer themselves as victims of reparation,

2. Louis de Montfort, *The Secret of Mary* (Charlotte, N.C.: TAN Books, 1998), p. 18.

saying that she was ready to lead them safely to God. And behold, they see a light shining from her maternal hands which penetrates them inwardly, so that they feel immersed in God just as—they explain—a person sees himself in a mirror.[3]

Little Francisco, recalling this experience later, said: "'We were burning in that light which is God and we were not consumed. What is God like? It is impossible to say. In fact, we will never be able to tell people.'"[4]

They were plunged into the fire of divine love. This is a fire that illuminates, not destroys, a fire that warms us, full of ardor and life. The pope then made a comparison with Moses' experience of the burning bush: "Moses had the same experience when he saw God in the burning bush; he heard God say that he was concerned about the slavery of his people and had decided to deliver them through him: 'I will be with you' (cf. Ex 3:2–12). Those who welcome this presence become the dwelling place—and consequently, a 'burning bush'—of the Most High."[5]

It's deeply moving to see how these young children of Fatima, while still ignorant of so much, had in the

---

3. John Paul II, *Homily at the Beatification of Francisco and Jacinta Marto, Shepherds of Fatima*, 13 May 2000, 1, *www.vatican.va*.

4. Ibid.

5. Ibid.

end experienced something similar to the experience of so important a figure in the story of salvation as Moses. Through Mary, they entered into a very profound experience of the living God. We should not be jealous. We are without a doubt not living sensibly through the same things. Yet in the domain of faith, all, least and greatest, can attain the same realities and know God, thus becoming "burning bushes of the Almighty" and sharing God's compassion that desires to liberate his people.

CHAPTER 12

Touching God in Prayer

I am more and more convinced of the essential place of prayer in the Christian life. What the world needs most today are people who are in real and profound communion with God through prayer. All genuine improvements come from prayer. St. Peter of Alcántara, a friend of Teresa of Avila, said: "In prayer, the soul cleanses itself from sin, charity is nourished, faith is strengthened, hope is made secure, the spirit rejoices, the soul grows tender, and the heart is purified; truth discovers itself, temptation is overcome, sadness takes to flight, the senses are renewed, failing virtue is made good, tepidity disappears, the rust of sin is rubbed away. In it are brought forth lively flashes of heavenly desires, and in these fires rises the flame of divine love."[1]

---

1. Peter of Alcántara, *Treatise on Prayer and Meditation* (Charlotte, N.C.: TAN Books, 2008), p. 7.

The Church and the world are living through difficult times, but God is faithful. He reveals himself and
communicates himself to those who seek him and want
him. St. John of the Cross wrote in the sixteenth century:
"The Lord has always revealed to mortals the treasures of
his wisdom and his spirit, but now that the face of evil
bares itself more and more, so does the Lord bare his treasures more."[2] What would he say today?

Prayer is Faith, Hope, and Love

What is needed to have a fruitful prayer life, one that
really allows for an encounter with God and transforms
our life little by little? St. John of the Cross said there are
people who think they pray well but pray poorly, and others who think they pray poorly but pray very well.[3] Where
does the difference lie? What puts us truly in communion
with God in prayer?

In the time we devote to prayer, we can do diverse
things: recite the Rosary, meditate on a passage of Scripture, ruminate slowly on a psalm, dialogue freely with the
Lord, or remain silently in his presence.

---

2. John of the Cross, *Sayings of Light and Love*, 1 in *The Collected Works of St. John
of the Cross*, p. 44.

3. John of the Cross, *Ascent of Mt. Carmel*, trans E. Allison Peers (New York: Burns
& Oates, 2001), Prologue.

But what is decisive in the end is not this or that method, such and such an activity, but the deep disposition of our hearts while we are in prayer. These profound dispositions are nothing other than faith, hope, and love. All the rest is included in these attitudes, expressing them, nourishing them, maintaining them.

Faith Suffices

"The greater is the faith of the soul, the more closely it is united to God."[4]

Sometimes while praying, we have agreeable feelings of peace and happiness, a sensation of the presence of God. We also may receive enlightenment regarding some aspect of the mystery of Christ or intuitions of what God expects from us. These graces that move our senses or enlighten our intelligence are very precious, and we must welcome them in recognition that they are a kind of food and an encouragement for faith and love.

Even so, they are not the essence of what brings us closer to God and places us in communion with him. In fact, God is infinitely beyond all we can know with our senses or perceive with our intelligence. When the senses are in a dry spell and the intelligence is darkened, we

---

4. John of the Cross, *Ascent of Mt. Carmel*, p. 93.

should never be discouraged or feel far from God. What ensures, what gives rise to, contact with God are neither feelings nor rational knowledge, but an act of faith. "I will betroth you to me in faithfulness; and you shall know the Lord." (Hos 2:20).

From the moment I make a sincere and real act of hope (a loving, confident hope, desiring to give myself to God), I can be certain of being in touch with God, no matter what positive or disagreeable emotions I may happen to be feeling or what thoughts, whether light or dark, fill my mind. St. John of the Cross often insisted that faith suffices for someone united to God, a great consolation indeed.

Sometimes when we feel very low, we have the sense of being far from God, even though a simple act of faith would be enough to stir up absolute certainty of being in profound communion with him, communion that sooner or later will bring the fruits of interior transformation—a faith simultaneously consisting of both total confidence in God and full adherence to what he reveals to us of himself through the Scriptures and the Church.

On this let me quote words of a Dominican sister who died in 1980, Sister Marie de la Trinité. For a long time she lived with a profound experience of God, of his fatherhood in particular, yet all the while undergoing painful psychological suffering. These two texts show the fundamental role of faith in giving us access to the mystery of God through the person of Christ.

> This is given to me like the wings of the great eagle of the Apocalypse (Rv 12:14), which carries me as it were to the limit of faith, toward what eye has not seen, nor ear heard, nor heart felt. Nor do I see, hear, experience, but the gift of faith goes infinitely further, leading to the reality that infinitely surpasses any humanly accessible reality. Faith leads us to Him who gives it, well beyond all experience or personal conviction, beyond even what love would dare, if God were not present at the very mystery of his own love.[5]

> I saw that faith imbued with love makes us attain this other side [the profound depth of the life of the Trinity], not through Christ and in him, but drawing us into it as he himself resides in it. And I was there myself through his mercy, and in faith embedded with love—and I saw how near at hand it is![6]

---

5. Christiane Sanson, *Marie de la Trinité: de l'angoisse à la paix* (Paris: Les Éditions du Cerf, 2005), p. 279.

6. Marie de la Trinité, *Consens à n'être rien* (Paris: Éditions Arfuyen, 2002), p. 57.

Faith and Touch

One could make an interesting connection between the role of faith in the spiritual life and the role of the sense of touch in the life of the senses. Among the five senses at our command, touch is the first to be developed starting even at our mother's bosom, and it forms the point of origin for all the others. It doesn't have the richness of some of the other senses, like vision (with all the diversity of images that we can ponder) or hearing (encountering the variety of sounds, melodies). It is the most primordial but the most essential sense in life and in communication. And it possesses an advantage other senses don't have: reciprocity. We can see without being seen, hear without being heard, but we can't touch an object without being touched by it at the same time. The contact that comes with touching something is more intimate and immediate than that created by any other sense. It is par excellence, the sense of communion.

In a similar way, faith has certain obvious limitations (one does not "have faith in" what is seen or heard or otherwise apprehended by the senses), yet it is also what is most vital in the spiritual life. Through faith, we can, in a mysterious but real way, *touch God* and let ourselves be touched by him, establishing ourselves in intimate communion with him and allowing ourselves to be transformed, little by little, by his grace.

CHAPTER 13

Teresa of Avila
and the Interior Castle

In 2015, we celebrated the fifth centennial of the birth of Teresa of Avila (born March 28, 1515). Her feast day, October 15th, began the "Teresa of Avila Year," inviting us to reflect anew on the message of the holy reformer of Carmel, which remains so essential for our world. The first time I read her autobiography, many years ago, it was like a spiritual electric shock.

The gospel for her feast day Mass, according to the Carmelite rite, is taken from chapter 4 of the Book of John. It is the story of the Jesus' encounter with the Samaritan woman by the well of Jacob at Sychar (Jn 4:1–30). The choice of this reading invites us to open ourselves to the richness of God's love—if *we* knew the gift of God!—and find in Jesus this pure, living, flowing water, that alone can quench our infinite thirst for true love. In her writings, Teresa of Avila often used the image of water to symbolize divine grace found principally through prayer.

> There came a woman of Samaria to draw water. Jesus said to her, "Give me a drink." For his disciples had gone away into the city to buy food. The Samaritan woman said to him, "How is it that you, a Jew, ask a drink of me, a woman of Samaria?" For Jews have no dealings with Samaritans. Jesus answered her, "If you knew the gift of God, and who it is that is saying to you, 'Give me a drink,' you would have asked him, and he would have given you living water." The woman said to him, "Sir, you have nothing to draw with, and the well is deep; where do you get that living water? Are you greater than our father Jacob, who gave us the well, and drank from it himself, and his sons, and his cattle?" Jesus said to her, "Every one who drinks of this water will thirst again, but whoever drinks of the water that I shall give him will never thirst; the water that I shall give him will become in him a spring of water welling up to eternal life." (Jn 4:7–14)

This magnificent gospel gives us a dialogue between Jesus, true source of living water, and a woman thirsty for love, as we all are. The dialogue expresses two thirsts. One is the thirst of Jesus: "Give me a drink!" . . . God's surprising thirst of love for his creature, a thirst that will be expressed in its supreme manner on the Cross: "I thirst!" (Jn 19:28). Jesus thirsts to give us the living water of his love. And here before him is the second unexpressed but very real thirst of this woman who has sought love all her life in a chaotic manner, it would seem, involving five successive marriages and a sixth man with whom she lives now.

Meditating on this passage, I was struck by the woman's words: "The well is deep!"

This is the depth of God's love for us, and also of our desire, our need for love. Teresa of Avila was so overcome by this thirst that she was convinced that if she remained in this world she would certainly be lost. This is why she decided to become a nun: to assuage her need to love. After several years of searching, of hesitation, and of painful struggles, one day before a little statue of suffering Jesus, she received a revelation of the infinite love of the Crucified, finding in him the freedom to love and be loved as much as her heart desired, even as she felt regret at having felt so little gratitude toward him.

How large the heart of God is, and how large also the heart of mankind—so large in its desire, its thirst, that nothing in this world can satisfy it, yet large also in all that it discovers within when it lets itself be seized by

God's love. One of Teresa of Avila's most precious teach-
ings is to show us by the image of the "Interior Castle"
just how spacious the human soul is, how many rooms
and secret chambers it contains—what a vast world of
extraordinary variety and richness is found within the
soul, created in the image of God and dwelling place of
the Trinity. The center of the soul is God, St. John of the
Cross said. The drama of mankind, as St. Augustine saw,
comes from its too often looking outside itself for what it
already possesses within. That God dwells in the human
soul was something Teresa did not grasp for a long time,
but having received the grace of conversion, she woke
with wonder to the divine presence in her heart, and to
contemplation, until then so difficult for her.

This lesson is vital today. We are people dying from
thirst while next to a well, in our anguish, fatigue, and
blindness, running after a thousand things outside us
while untold riches within us await discovery. We possess
within ourselves a kingdom more vast than the universe.
All that we desire is already present in the depths of our
hearts where God resides, ready to give us all.

How do we gain access to this kingdom within us?
Teresa answers: faithfulness to prayer. The way isn't always
easy. Our hearts are like old wells, filled with rocks, debris,
dead leaves, trash. Going down there means accepting the

painful truth that what resides in us is often wounded or dirty. But if we don't get discouraged and are faithful to our personal prayer, seeking God's presence within us through an act of faith, we shall discover the spring flowing in our inmost depths: pure, nurturing, sweet, peaceful, and refreshing. There in our hearts, we shall drink at the source of the living waters of God's love and, having been changed and purified, become able to quench the thirst for the love of those whom the Lord has placed along our way. "The water that I shall give him will become in him a spring of water welling up to eternal life" (Jn 4:14).

May Teresa of Avila give us determination and courage in our faithfulness to prayer and lead us to these living waters that she knew.

For those who wish to meditate further on God's presence within us, see the following spiritual references.

Chapter 28 in Teresa of Ávila, *The Way of Perfection*, trans E. Allison Peers (New York: Image Books, 2004).

John of the Cross, *Spiritual Canticle*, B 1.6–8 in *The Spiritual Canticle & Poems*, trans. E. Allison Peers (New York: Burns & Oates, 1978), pp. 196–197.

Teresa Benedicta of the Cross (Edith Stein), *The Science of the Cross*, trans. Josephine Koeppel, OCD (Washington, D.C.: ICS Publications, 2003).

CHAPTER 14

Etty Hillesum,
Witness of Hope

I n 1981, long excerpts from a young Jewish girl's journal, written between March 1942 and June 1943, were published in their original language, Dutch. The writer, from Amsterdam, was deported to Auschwitz and disappeared there. Although the journal excerpts relate the story of something that happened close to forty years before they were published, the publication was a huge success. It was followed by translations in various languages (including French in 1985). That is how the name and spiritual itinerary of Etty (Esther) Hillesum came to be known.

Since then, her renown and influence have grown unceasingly, a sign of how revolutionary and meaningful the interior life to which Etty's journal (and letters) testify is for men and women of today. Her work, of great literary quality, is increasingly recognized as a major memoir of the twentieth century, destined to be a big influence on our times. Very close to us in her sensibilities, her aspirations, her freedom, and also her wandering, Etty, in less than three years, underwent a spiritual transformation that brought her to a surprising interior maturity and freedom, as well as a remarkable blossoming in the love of God and gift of self.

A Scattered Life

When Etty began her journal, she was twenty-seven years old. She lived in Amsterdam, but she had spent her childhood in Deventer where her parents still lived. Her father, Louis Hillesum, ran a middle school. He was an erudite soul, whose amiable and resigned humor hid the difficulty he had facing life. His wife, Riva (Rebecca) Bernstein, was a Jew who emigrated from Russia in 1907, of a fantastical and domineering temperament. Family life seems not to have been very harmonious, and Etty's relationship with her parents was difficult. She was the eldest of three children. Her closest brother, Jaap, was two years younger. Though interested in medicine, he was psychologically fragile and spent several intervals in psychiatric institutes. The second sibling, Mischa, eight years younger than Etty, would become a talented pianist, but he also was psychologically fragile. They were an assimilated Jewish family, who maintained ties with Judaism but didn't eat kosher or observe the Sabbath. Etty didn't know very much about the traditions of Israel.

When she began her journal, Etty lived in Amsterdam, having come there for legal and literary studies. She was a lively, intelligent, warm, and spontaneous young woman, full of humor and idealistic, but with the exaggerated character of her mother. Her life was far from orderly. She suffered from some physical maladies (while suspecting they weren't entirely of physical origin), while her passionate temperament and idealism led her to throw herself into a number of relationships that left her "unhappy and torn up." After living in various student lodgings, she moved in 1937 into a house close to the Rijksmuseum. Her landlord, Han Wegerif, a retired widower, had engaged her to take care of his household, which besides himself was composed of a servant and two students, including his youngest son. Etty fell rather quickly into a relationship with Han that lasted five years. She took care of the house, studied Russian, and did some tutoring.

A Providential Encounter

In February of 1941, Etty had a life-changing encounter with Julius Spier, a Jew from Berlin who had immigrated to Holland. He was fifty-four years old; Etty was twenty-seven. Formerly the director of a bank, he had dedicated himself to psychology under the influence of Carl Jung, the famous Swiss psychiatrist.

Spier, who had a knack for helping unsettled people find equilibrium and tranquility, gave Etty advice and exercises that proved very beneficial. She met with him regularly, entering into his circle of intimate friends and becoming his secretary.

At first the relationship was not without ambiguity. Etty still had a strong tendency to desire those she admired in an erotic way. As for Spier, he was a profoundly good and intelligent man—and, little by little, became a believer—but one who had difficulty mastering his sexuality. But their relationship evolved to become a beautiful friendship, free and respectful. From this encounter, Etty began to be profoundly transformed. Troubled at first, she wanted to undertake the task of diligently "working on" herself with courage and putting her life in order.[1]

She began to write her journal on the eighth of March. It brought precious human and spiritual advancement for her, and, giving focus to her need for lucidity and her determination to try to see clearly through her

---

1. All quotes in this chapter are taken from the book by Etty Hillesum, *Etty: The Letters and Diaries of Etty Hillesum, 1941–1943*, ed. Klaas A. D. Smelik, trans. Arnold J. Pomerans (Grand Rapids, MI: William B. Eerdmans, 2002).

inner struggles; it permitted her to clarify and deepen the intuitions that slowly began to orient and unify her life. The journal would also become her preferred way to express and intensify the dialogue that she was gradually establishing with God.

Without adhering to any particular religious creed and while remaining very modest in his interior life, Spier also had gone through a remarkable spiritual journey. An agnostic, his contact with Jung led him to be interested in religion. He rediscovered the Bible, the Gospels, and Christian authors, and he entered into a relationship with God and a kind of prayer life.

Through contact with him, Etty herself also discovered the Word of God. She began to read the Bible, the Psalms, the Gospels (especially the Gospel of Matthew), and the letters of Paul. She also read St. Augustine and Thomas à Kempis' *The Imitation of Christ*. The influence of Tolstoy, of Dostoyevsky, and in particular, of the poet Rainer Maria Rilke, whom Etty quoted frequently, were also important.

Little by little, she who was very far from any creed began to pronounce the name of God. The "girl who could not kneel" found herself more and more regularly in this humble posture, as often in the bathroom as in the jumble of her room.

Meditating head in hands, she often found strength and peace in prayer, and gradually she entered into a free and spontaneous, but very intimate and profound, dialogue with God—a God who remained very mysterious, but whose presence she felt profoundly. She said, "There is a really deep well inside me. And in it dwells God. Sometimes I am there, too. But more often stones and grit block the well, and God is buried beneath. Then He must be dug out again." She identified God with what was most profound within herself, with a need for permanent interior attentiveness.

Life Is Beautiful and Full of Meaning

As she was attaining this courage to pronounce the name of God and developing a need to listen to her personal interiority, Etty more and more felt an unconditional love of life being born in her. She was discovering life to be beautiful and full of meaning. At the same time, paradoxically, the exterior life of Jews in Holland was becoming worse and worse. They were wearing the yellow star, confined to a ghetto, enduring limits on freedoms, forbidden to walk in public gardens, and suffering food restrictions, with vexations and humiliations constantly raining down. And here is the most surprising aspect of

Etty's spiritual journey: the more the world around her
grew dark and burdensome, the more her exterior freedom was stifled, so much the more did she find herself
a peaceful space, of freedom, an immense love of life, of
God, of every creature.

Here is one of the many passages that testifies to this:

This morning, in going by bicycle along the Stadion-
kade, I was enchanted by the vast horizon you find at
the edge of the city and I was breathing the fresh air
that hasn't yet been rationed for us. There were notices
all over forbidding Jews from using the little paths
that lead into nature. But at this end of the road that
was left open to us the sky spread out entirely. They
couldn't do anything about this, really nothing. They
could make life rather hard for us, deprive us of certain good products, take away from us a certain freedom of exterior movement, but we're the ones who
deprive ourselves of our best forces by a disastrous
psychological attitude, by feeling ourselves persecuted,
humiliated, oppressed. By feeling hate. By showing
off to hide our fear. We certainly have the right to be
sad and beaten down from time to time by what they
make us go through: it's human and understandable.
And yet, the real dispossession is inflicted by ourselves.
I find life to be so beautiful and I feel free. In me the

sky extends as far as the heavens. I believe in God and I believe in mankind, I dare to say it without false timidity. . . . I am a happy woman and I sing the praises of this life—yes, you have read right—in the year of grace 1942, the umpteenth year of the war.

In Etty's view, "We may suffer, but we must not succumb." This love of life that unfolds in Etty is not some naive romanticism or a flight from reality. Quite the contrary. It is a welcoming of reality just as it is, to the acceptance of all that life offers, without exception: the joys as well as the pains, happiness and suffering, the sweetness of a moment of friendship as well as the prospect of a separation.

Seeing how many people reacted to the difficulties of her time with fear and anguish, while focusing on saving their skins at all costs (sometimes even at the cost of someone else's skin), Etty was acutely aware that the real problem in human life isn't so much suffering itself as the fear it inspires due to our inability to accept it and assume it. The worry to which suffering gives rise does more harm than the suffering itself.

Etty forced herself (through the highs and the lows!) moment by moment to accept as good everything life brought her. "From your hands, my God, I accept everything, as it comes. It is always good, I know it. I have learned that in putting up with all the trials we can turn

them to good. . . . Always, as soon as I show myself
ready to face them, the trials have changed into beauty."

Living Like the Lilies of the Field

In her reading of the Gospel and her sharing with Julius
Spier, Etty was taken by the teaching of Jesus on abandon-
ing oneself to Providence. The desire to live like "the lilies
of the field" (Mt 6:28) became a leitmotif of her interior
life. The daily struggles were often rather difficult during
this troubled time; all the more necessary to put the gospel into practice. As worries threatened to overcome Etty
without end in sight, she found within herself a fierce
determination to abandon herself to the will of God and
trust deeply in him, telling herself that she had no right to
worry about the future.

She understood very clearly how necessary it is to
avoid worry, which gnaws on us and prevents us from
being open to the grace and beauty present in each
moment of life, how important it is to keep ourselves
from burdening the present days with grief from the
weight of anxieties about tomorrow.

> When we project in advance our worry for all sorts
> of things to come, we prevent them from developing

organically. I have in me an immense confidence. Not a certainty of seeing external life go well for me, but of continuing to accept life and to find it good, even in the worst moments.

In September 1942, Etty wrote:

Let me just note down one more thing for myself: Matthew 6:34: "Take therefore no thought for the morrow: for the morrow shall take thought for the things of itself. Sufficient unto the day is the evil thereof." We have to fight them daily, like fleas, those many small worries about the morrow, for they sap our energy. We make mental provision for the days to come, and everything turns out differently, quite differently. Sufficient unto the day. The things that have to be done must be done, and for the rest we must not allow ourselves to become infested with thousands of petty fears and worries, so many motions of no confidence in God. Everything will turn out all right.

Employee of the Jewish Council

In January 1942, during the conference of the Reich's leaders in Wannsee, the *final solution* was decreed: the extermination of the Jews in Europe. The roundups multiplied; everywhere the sinister railroad convoys carried loads of victims toward the extermination camps. The process was begun in Holland at the beginning of July 1942.

Pressured by friends, Etty accepted a position as employee of the "Jewish Council" (a group supposedly responsible for managing the interests of the Jewish community, but without any real power against the Nazis, which at least at first assured her relative security.) This privileged situation was repugnant to her, and she only accepted it with the thought that she would be able to use it to give consolation and encouragement to her fellow Jews in troubled times. It was exacting office work, in a climate of anguish and panic. But Etty was able to preserve her freedom, her peace, her relationship with God, and her love of life there.

> The exterior threat and terror increases day by day. I raise up prayer around me like a protective wall full of protective shadows. I retire in prayer as if in the cell of a convent, and I come out more concentrated, stronger, more collected.

She was ecstatic at the discovery of a jasmine plant that blossomed in front of her window, and at a bouquet of roses that she found after a harassing day at work.

My red and yellow roses are all opened. While I was down there, in hell, they continued to flower very sweetly. Many are those who say to me: how can you still dream of flowers? . . . They're all there. They aren't less real than all the distress I witness in a day. There is room in my life for a lot of things.

Until the end, Etty remained capable of accepting the beauty of nature as a word of hope and encouragement. She also remained able to savor her friendships, to give thanks for a meeting, a moment spent with a loved one. At the same time her love, so devouring before, while still remaining very intense, made her freer and more detached, more universal also, more capable of reaching out toward any human being without exception, good or bad, worthy or unworthy of this love. She understood that concern for loved ones, if legitimate, should never become a barrier to opening one's heart to all those around us, whoever they may be. In fact, Etty felt that it was essential to reserve all one's strength, love, and trust in God, instead of wasting it on worry, so that there would be plenty for those who might need it later on.

She also felt that, little by little, she should become detached from everything, that nothing should get in the way of freely following the destiny that was hers, to say goodbye perhaps to familiar places in order to share in the lot of her people.

> When we begin to renounce these must-haves and these desires, we can also renounce everything. I've learned this in the space of a couple days. . . . Each day I say goodbye. The real goodbye won't be anything more than a little external confirmation of what was accomplished in me day by day.

She accepted the prospect of death:

> The eventuality of death is integrated into my life; looking at death straight on and accepting it as an integral part of life, is to enlarge life. The opposite would be to sacrifice from now on a piece of this life to death, out of fear of death and refusing to accept it; that's the best way to keep only a little bit of a poor, mutilated life, barely deserving of such a name. It seems like a paradox: in excluding death from one's life we deny ourselves a complete life and in welcoming it we enlarge and enrich our life.

Westerbork

The Dutch Jews arrested by the Nazis all wound up staying in the police transit camp of Westerbork, situated on the uncultivated moor in Drenthe, in the northeast of the Netherlands. About 100,000 Dutch Jews, including Edith Stein, would pass through this camp between July 1942 and September 1944. It was from there that a convoy of at least 1,000 people left every Tuesday for an unknown destination in the East. Most often it was going to Auschwitz. Ann Frank and her family were in the last convoy.

The Jewish Council maintained a branch in the camp, a sort of "social service." Etty asked to be sent there, thinking she would be more useful there than in Amsterdam. She arrived at the beginning of August 1942. She remained free to leave the camp, and she returned to Amsterdam three times for visits of various lengths until at last the Nazi noose tightened on all the Jews without exception; she was imprisoned definitively in July 1943.

Except for overcrowding, material conditions at Westerbork weren't too stark. It was mainly the climate of uncertainty about the future, the anguishing question hanging in the air of who would be on the next convoy, the anxiety to avoid being on the next list that created an atmosphere of tension, of debilitating insecurity. Many persons of great social importance previously— artists, jurists, rich and famous people—found themselves powerless.

Now we perceive that it doesn't suffice in life to be an able politician or talented artist. As soon as we reach the bottom of distress, life demands other qualities. Yes, it's true, we are judged by the measuring stick of our ultimate human values.

By the time of Etty's second return to Amsterdam, in September 1942, Julius Spier had fallen gravely ill, and she was present at his death. Etty accepted this immense loss with calm. Ready to go on alone, she gave thanks for the gift that this friend had been.

You are the one who freed up these forces within me that are at my disposition. You taught me to say the name of God without shame. You served as a mediator between God and me, but now, you the mediator, you have retired and my path leads henceforth directly to God; it's good this way and I know it. And I, also, will serve as a mediator for all those whom I can help.

A Refusal to Hate

Faced with the terrifying and cruel injustice inflicted on the Jews by the Nazis, Etty was sometimes tempted to react like many of her contemporaries with despair, or by revolting, or with hate. As for despair, we have seen how she had been immunized by her confidence in God. Very lucidly, she also detected what was often false in the attitude of revolt that rose up in one or another of those close to her, feeling that many people were only indignant about the injustices if they themselves were the victims of them.

As for hate, Etty was of course tempted to hate the Germans. But she quickly understood that hate is a terrible poison in the heart of the one who feels it. If she nourished hate for her persecutor, the innocent victim of an injustice would herself enter into the spiral of evil and become complicit in it. At the end of a long, moving letter describing the situation at the transit camp of Westerbork, realizing that she had given an accurate account of the atrocious reality that nevertheless was without bitterness and hate, she said:

> This is a very subjective picture. I understand that one could give a different version involving more hatred, bitterness, and rebellion. But the rebellion that waits to be born the moment something bad touches you personally has nothing authentic about it and will never be fruitful. . . . And the absence of hatred doesn't necessarily mean an absence of an elementary moral indignation. I know that those who hate have good reasons for doing so. But why should we always

choose the easiest path, the most traveled? In camp, I feel with all my being that the least atom of hatred added to this world makes it still more inhospitable. And I think, with perhaps a childlike but tenacious naïveté, that if this earth one day will become more inhabitable again only through the love that the Jew Paul described to the residents of Corinth in the thirteenth chapter of his first letter.

Here we see the maturity Etty had attained. Far from calling forth bitterness and hate, her confrontation with evil was lived as an invitation to react with an abundance of love and to recognize that the roots of evil are in each one of us. That is where we must fight it first.

The filth in others is also in us. And I don't see any other solution, any other solution at all, except to enter into oneself and uproot all that is rotten from our soul. I no longer believe that we can correct anything in the exterior world that we haven't yet corrected in ourselves. The only lesson that this war has taught us is to look into ourselves and not elsewhere.

She forced herself to recognize that behind even a persecutor was a human being, with his own interior void, his own distress, and to apply the gospel precept of love of enemies as well as the word of Paul to the Romans:

"Do not be overcome by evil, but overcome evil by good" (Rm 12:21).

Some would say this is a difficult, unrealistic and vain attitude. But how else can we stop the spiral of evil? Resentment and hate only feed and propagate evil; only unconditional love of all humankind can put an end to it.

Wanting to Be a Balm Poured Out onto So Many Wounds

At Westerbork, Etty felt called to the mission: of being the "thinking heart of the hovel"—filled with lucid and rational love and extending compassion to all those she touched. At the heart of this unspeakable distress, she sought to be a presence of peace and comfort through the material aid she could furnish, the letters she ensured got sent, some encouraging words, or her mere presence when words failed. She spent herself selflessly as a companion to mothers, children who were alone, elderly persons—all those for whom she could provide a little comfort. Her attitude at the camp was the unfailing sign of the authenticity of her spiritual experience. The convictions formed at Amsterdam, the peace and interior freedom she discovered there, did not fade away but were only strengthened.

The fields of the soul and the spirit are so vast, so infinite, that this little cup of discomfort and physical suffering has little importance, I don't have the impression of being deprived of my freedom and, in the end, no one can really do me harm.

Her prayer life also grew deeper. "Sometimes when I stand in some corner of the camp, my feet planted on Your earth, my eyes raised toward Your heaven, tears sometimes run down my face—the only outlet of my interior emotion and my gratitude . . . and it's my prayer."

Helping God

This unusual expression "help God" comes several times from Etty's pen, especially when she is cruelly reminded of all the suffering parading before her.

I am going to help you, my God, in not letting you be extinguished in me, but I can't guarantee anything in advance. One thing, though, seems clearer and clearer to me: it's not you who can help us, but we who can help you—and in doing so we help ourselves. What we can save at these times is also the only thing that counts: a little bit of you in us, my God. Perhaps we can also contribute to bringing you to light in the martyrized hearts of others. . . . With each passing heartbeat it seems

more and more clear to me that you can't help us, but
that it's up to us to help you and to defend the place in
us where you dwell until the end.

What lies behind this unconventional prayer? Etty
wasn't doubting God's help; she'd had sufficient experience of it in the peace and strength that had been given
to her. But at this particular time, when God seemed to
be drawing back, remaining silent and seemingly powerless before the explosion of evil, she deemed it untimely
to demand her rights or request outside intervention. She
felt she must look to her own resources to keep her convictions alive within her (and to impart them to others to
the extent she could), and in others to "save," as it were, a
place for God—a place of peace, benevolence, humanity.
She asked the rhetorical question: "Will we let the flame
of good will and hope be extinguished by this system of
evil, or will we try to keep it alive, no matter the cost?"

The Last Trip

The Nazis' policies grew harsher. Etty resisted the advice
of friends who urged her to flee or hide. On what grounds
should she reject her share in the destiny of all? She
desired to participate in the fate of her people. Hadn't
she written while still free: "This little fragment of the

destiny of many that I am in a position to assume—I take it on my back like a bundle to which I am bound by knots ever stronger and tighter. I am one with it, and I bear it through the streets." Another reason for her choice was that her parents (whom she had newly learned to love after her interior evolution) as well as her brother Mischa had themselves been imprisoned at Westerbork since the great roundup of June 1943.

In July 1943, the members of the Jewish Council remaining at Westerbork were dispossessed of their special status, and Etty lost the possibility of leaving the camp, becoming a "resident" (though in principle not subject to deportation). Mischa, because of his well-known musical talents, had a chance to avoid being deported, but he didn't want to take advantage of it without his family. Actions like this appeared to the Nazis to be acts of defiance that angered them. On September 6 it was decided that all members of the Hillesum family would be deported. The camp commander included Etty in this order.

And so it was that the four members of the family imprisoned at Westerbork embarked on the convoy of September 7, leaving for Auschwitz. The Hillesums boarded the train very calmly and courageously. They were singing. Mischa and his parents were in the first car, Etty in number twelve. Etty brought her little backpack with her, filled with some personal effects. She had stuffed her journal, a Russian grammar book, some works of Tolstoy, and the Bible inside. She took the time to dash off two cards to say goodbye to friends, which she threw onto the track through an opening in the train car. Some country people found them and mailed them. One of them is preserved. It begins with these words: "Christine, I opened the Bible by chance and fell upon this: 'the Lord is my fortress . . .'"

Louis and Rebecca Hillesum likely died during the trip or were gassed immediately upon their arrival. Etty would die November 30, 1943 (according to the Red Cross), and Mischa in March of 1944. Only Jaap was still in Amsterdam; he would be deported in 1945 to Bergen Belsen and die of typhus in April. The whole family was annihilated.

We don't know anything about the few weeks spent in Auschwitz. But no doubt Etty had the grace of being faithful to the fundamental direction of her life: "I am ready to accept everything, every place on earth where it will please God to send me, ready also to witness through all situations until death, of the beauty and meaning of this life."

Works Cited

Benedict XVI. *Homily for the Closing of the 24th Italian National Eucharistic Congress.* 29 May 2005. *www.vatican.va.*

Benedict XVI. *Homily to France on the Occasion of the 150th Anniversary of the Apparitions of the Blessed Virgin Mary at Lourdes.* 15 September 2008. *www.vatican.va.*

Bernard of Clairvaux. *Bernard of Clairvaux: Monastic Sermons.* Collegeville, Minn.: Liturgical Press, 2016.

Daoust, J. *Le message eucharistique de Mère Mectilde du Saint Sacrement.* Paris: Téqui, 1979.

de Bar, Catherine. à l'écoute de saint Benoît. Rouen: Bénédictines du Saint-Sacrement, 1979.

de Bar, Catherine. *Adorer et Adhérer.* Paris: Éditions du Cerf, 1994.

de Montfort, Louis. *The Secret of Mary.* Charlotte, N.C.: TAN Books, 1998.

Francis. *The Infinite Tenderness of God.* Frederick, Md.: The Word Among Us, 2016.

Geneviève of the Holy Face (Céline Martin). *My Sister Saint Thérèse.* Charlotte, N.C.: TAN Books, 1997. E-book.

Guibert, Joël. *Renaître d'en haut: Une vie renouvelée par l'Esprit Saint.* Paris: Éditions de l'Emmanuel, 2008.

Hatzidakis, Emmanual. *The Heavenly Banquet: Understanding the Divine Liturgy*. Clearwater, Fla.: Orthodox Witness, 2013.

Hillesum, Etty. *Etty: The Letters and Diaries of Etty Hillesum, 1941–1943*. Edited by Klaas A. D. Smelik. Translated by Arnold J. Pomerans. Grand Rapids, Mich.: William B. Eerdmans, 2002.

John of the Cross. *Dark Night of the Soul*. Mineola, N.Y.: Dover, 2003.

John of the Cross. *The Ascent of Mount Carmel*. Translated by E. Allison Peers. New York: Burns & Oates, 2001.

John of the Cross. *The Collected Works of St. John of the Cross*. Translated by Kieran Kavanaugh, OCD, and Otilio Rodriguez, OCD. Washington. D.C.: ICS, 1991. Kindle edition.

John of the Cross. *The Spiritual Canticle & Poems*. Translated by E. Allison Peers. New York: Burns & Oates, 1978.

John Paul II. *Ecclesia de Eucharistia*. Encyclical on the Eucharist in Its Relationship to the Church. 17 April 2013. *www.vatican.va*.

John Paul II. *Homily at the Beatification of Francisco and Jacinta Marto, Shepherds of Fatima*. 13 May 2000. *www.vatican.va*.

John Paul II. *Homily to Priests on Holy Thursday 2005. www.vatican.va*.

John Paul II. *Mane Nobiscum Domine*. Apostolic Letter to the Bishops, Clergy, and Faithful for the Year of the Eucharist. 7 October 2004. *www.vatican.va*.

Kowalska, Faustina. *Diary of Saint Maria Faustina Kowalska: Divine Mercy in My Soul*. Stockbridge, Mass.: Marian Press, 2014.

Leinenweber, John. *Love One Another. My Friends: Saint Augustine's Homilies on the First Letter of John*. Eugene, Or.: Wipf & Stock, 1989.

Marie de la Trinité. *Consens à n'être rien*. Paris: Éditions Arfuyen, 2002.

Myers, Glenn E. *Seeking Spiritual Intimacy: Journeying Deeper with Medieval Women of Faith*. Downers Grove, Ill.: InterVarsity Press, 2011.

Peter of Alcántara. *Treatise on Prayer and Meditation*. Charlotte, N.C.: TAN Books, 2008.

Philippe, Jacques. *Searching for and Maintaining Peace: A Small Treatise on Peace of Heart*. Translated by George and Jannie Driscoll. Staten Island, N.Y.: Society of St. Paul, 2002. Kindle edition.

Sagne, Jean-Claude. *L'itinéraire spirituel du couple: Le Mystère de l'amour dans le marriage*. Saint-Paul: Chemin-Nouf, 2001.

Sanson, Christiane. *Marie de la Trinité: de l'angoisse à la paix*. Paris: Les Éditions du Cerf, 2005.

Scupoli, Lorenzo. *Spiritual Combat*. Manchester: R. W. Dean & Co, 1801.

Sommerfeldt, John R. *Erudition at God's Service*. Kalamazoo, Mich.: Cistercian Publications, 1987.

The Carthusian Order in England. *The Wound of Love: A Carthusian Miscellany*. Herefordshire: Gracewing, 2006.

The Fathers of the Church. Translated by Francis X. Glimm. Joseph M.-F. Marique, SJ, and Gerald G. Walsh, SJ. Washington, D.C.: The Catholic University of America Press, 2008.

Thérèse of Lisieux. *Letters of St. Thérèse of Lisieux, Volume I: 1877–1890.* Translated by John Clarke, OCD. Washington, D.C.: ICS, 1982. Kindle edition.

Thérèse of Lisieux. *St. Therese of Lisieux: Her Last Conversations.* Translated by John Clarke, OCD. Washington, D.C.: ICS, 1977.

Thérèse of Lisieux. *Story of a Soul: The Autobiography of St. Thérèse of Lisieux.* Translated by John Clarke, OCD. Washington, D.C.: ICS Publications, 1996. Kindle edition.

Thérèse of Lisieux. *The Poetry of Saint Thérèse of Lisieux.* Translated by Donald Kinney, OCD. Washington, D.C.: ICS Publications, 1995. Kindle edition.

Thérèse of Lisieux. *The Prayers of Saint Thérèse of Lisieux: The Act of Oblation.* Translated by Aletheia Kane, OCD. Washington, D.C.: ICS, 1997. Kindle edition.

Thérèse of Lisieux. *Letters of St. Thérèse of Lisieux, Volume II: 1890–1897.* Translated by John Clarke, OCD. Washington, D.C.: ICS, 1988. Kindle edition.